AF478150

The Legacy of Punishment in International Law

The Legacy of Punishment in International Law

Harry D. Gould

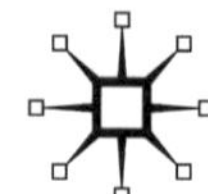

THE LEGACY OF PUNISHMENT IN INTERNATIONAL LAW
Copyright © Harry D. Gould, 2010.

First published in 2010 by PALGRAVE MACMILLAN® in the
United States - a division of St. Martin's Press LLC, 175 Fifth Avenue,
New York, NY 10010.

Where this book is distributed in the UK, Europe and the rest of the
World, this is by Palgrave Macmillan, a division of Macmillan
Publishers Limited, registered in England, company number 785998,
of Houndmills, Basingstoke, Hampshire RG21 6XS.

Palgrave Macmillan is the global academic imprint of the above
companies and has companies and representatives throughout the world.

Palgrave® and Macmillan® are registered trademarks in the United
States, the United Kingdom, Europe and other countries.

ISBN: 978–0–230–10438–9

Library of Congress Cataloging-in-Publication Data

Gould, Harry D.
    The legacy of punishment in international law / Harry D. Gould.
      p.   cm.
    Includes bibliographical references.
    ISBN 978–0–230–10438–9
    1. International law.   2. International offenses.   3. Punishment.
    I. Title.
    KZ3410.G676 2010
    341—dc22   2010007728

Design by Integra Software Services

First edition: September 2010

10 9 8 7 6 5 4 3 2 1

Printed in the United States of America.

For my family with deepest love

Contents

Acknowledgments

I hardly know where to begin in recognizing the wealth of assistance that has been rendered to me throughout the writing of this book. Although its direct ancestor was the dissertation I wrote under the supervision of Siba Grovogui in the Department of Political Science at the Johns Hopkins University, the roots extend much deeper. Having first been exposed to Kant's notion of the *categorical imperative* in John Clark's Ethics and International Relations seminar during my MA work in the Department of International Relations at Florida International University, I was positively astonished to find an apparently parallel legal concept, *jus cogens,* in Farrokh Jhabvala's International Law seminar. My interest in the idea of categorical obligation in international law comes from the early period of my MA coursework.

None of this, neither MA nor PhD nor completed book, could have happened without the generosity of the secretarial staffs at FIU and Johns Hopkins, and they all have my everlasting gratitude: Kathy Hasselbach, Mireille "Mimi" Sylvain-Davide, Martha Rodriguez, Michelle Real, Luz Aviles, Mary Cossio, Marge Collignon, Lisa Williams, Barbara Hall, and Kristin Szwajkowski.

Reaching back to my days as an undergraduate at New College of Florida, I would like to thank Dan McIntosh, who taught me to read IR and think IR, and Peggy Bates, who taught me (via lakes of red ink) to write IR.

During my doctoral studies, I was truly privileged to study with a number of marvelous faculty, all of whose fingerprints appear on this volume to one degree or another. Siba Grovgui and Dan Deudney built upon my previous work in IR Theory in their own courses, and guided me with wisdom and patience through the dissertation writing process. Dick Flathman and Bill Connolly turned me from an IR student with a taste for and curiosity about political theory into a member of the small but growing community of scholars working on international political theory. Working on moral philosophy with Jerry Schneewind allowed for the kind of close reading and analysis of philosophical texts that would benefit Ethics and IR as a field, and alleviate much of its unseemly philosophical superficiality. Anthony Pagden demonstrated the proper way to undertake work on the history of ideas, and his tremendous familiarity with the authors featured in Chapter 2 of this book has saved me from innumerable embarrassments. Finally, seminars on Roman Law undertaken with Robert Westbrook laid the foundation for much of the analysis of contemporary practices' roots in the *corpus juris civilis.*

Having returned to FIU as a member of the faculty, I have had the pleasure of working with very kind, supportive colleagues who have provided me with guidance and friendship: Francois Debrix, my tenure mentor; Majid Al-Khalili; Paul Kowert; Lisa Prügl; Tom Breslin, who was very generous in helping to translate passages of Latin that exceeded my meager knowledge; Antonio Jorge, who kindly read and commented upon every word of this manuscript; Claire Apodaca; Ralph Clem; Felix Martin; Rich Olson; John Stack; Nicol Rae; Mohiaddin Mesbahi; Ben Smith; Paul Warren; and Jin Zeng.

Teaching at FIU has also allowed me to work with some outstanding students, several of whom have helped me out at various stages of the drafting of this manuscript, and I must add none of them were ever my graduate assistant; they all read and commented on chapter drafts of their own generosity. Thank you to Amir Mirtaheri, Lisa Samuel, Christopher Brown, Mohammad Houmayounvash, Charles Heck, and Serena Cruz for your specific contributions to this book. More generally, I owe thanks to my grad students in IR Theory 1 and IR Theory 2, and my undergrads in The Development of IR Thought. The grad students heard my ruminations on state personality on numerous occasions, and my under-grad course helped shape my thoughts on the evolution of international punishment and its co-constitutive relationship with sovereignty. It was in the context of this undergrad course that I became acquainted with Richard Tuck's book *The Rights of War and Peace*. It was Professor Tuck's use of the theme of punishment that prompted my own reflections on the topic, and this work's debt to his book is readily apparent at multiple points.

The single greatest intellectual influence on my career generally, and this book particularly, has been Nick Onuf. It is my pleasure to have been—at various times—Nick's student, graduate assistant, colleague, and collaborator. Nick has read and commented on multiple drafts of everything that follows, and I have always benefitted from getting to read whatever Nick has been working on. I have completely lost track of the multitude of suggestions Nick has made that have shaped this book in fundamental ways: from its original (and my still-preferred) title, *Punishing Nations;* suggestions on how to frame a number of theoretical issues; solutions to theoretical problems; pointing out areas where my work duplicated earlier studies that, to my shame, I was unfamiliar with; and the rather unsexy task of fixing my clunky prose.

I am very grateful for the consistently challenging feed-back on my work that I have received from discussants and co-panelists over the last several years. In particular I would like to acknowledge the following people. Chris Brown, Tony Lang, Cecelia Lynch, Brent Steele, Eric Heinze, Jacque Amoureux, Jon Carlson, Michael Struett, Jonathan Havercroft and Kate Schick.

Although it's a bit awkward to mention, thanks must also be extended to Mike Campbell Joe and Ruthanne Ward, Shenna Perez-Martin, Vernon Savage, Sally Rowley, and Carlos Danger for keeping me functioning properly through all of this.

Finally, I gratefully acknowledge Cambridge University Press and the *Review of International Studies* for permission to reprint "International Criminal Bodies," which was an earlier version of Chapter 6, and Palgrave Macmillan for permission to reprint "What Happened to Punishment in the Just War Tradition," which, previously appeared as a chapter in Eric Heinze and Brent Steele eds, *Ethics, Authority and War* (2009) and parts of which appear in Chapter 2.

CHAPTER 1

Introduction

> The continued development of universality, objective norms such as norms *jus cogens*, obligations *erga omnes* and international crimes...all point to a move from strict positivism, absolute equality of consent and unanimity.[1]

In Nicholas Onuf's account of the constitution of international society, key explanatory weight is carried by two sets of constitutive rules that he labels "primary" and "secondary."[2] He takes this formulation from the system H. L. A. Hart detailed in *The Concept of Law*.[3] In the simplest terms, the former are the specific rules—prescriptive and prohibitive—governing the conduct of agents. The latter are rules governing rules—the rules for the creation and change of rules.[4] This typology neatly captures things, but there is a subspecies of primary rules that bears special attention for the unique role it plays in the constitution of international society—indeed of all societies. Among primary rules, rules of categorical, peremptory character, *jus cogens*, play a special role in the constitution of any society. More so than rules of a quotidian, dispositive character, *jus cogens* rules identify what it means to be part of a society. Adherence to these rules—if not *in foro interno* adherence to the values underlying them—is a *sine qua non* condition of membership in the society defined by those rules.

Even in a legal environment characterized by Positivism and Voluntarism (like international society), there are still some rules that are considered absolute.[5] Although categorical obligation is usually associated with Natural Law thinking or Kantian ethics, modern international law has found, or perhaps more accurately *created,* a place for peremptory obligation (to use international law's preferred term).[6]

International law's conceptualization of peremptory norms differs in important ways from that of both Natural Law and Kantian ethics. Unlike "Laws of Nature," *jus cogens* are human created, and they are subject to change. These rules are *made* by people, and they are *endowed* with their peremptory status by people. Unlike Kant's conception of categorical obligation, there is no *a priori* basis for the subject matter content of these rules or their peremptory character.[7] Instead, as stated previously, we *make* these rules categorical; we *make* certain prohibitions unconditional, and sometimes *make* certain positive obligations unconditional. The basis of categorical obligation in international law is rooted in neither Natural Law metaphysics, nor deontological reason; categorical obligation is a construction of human minds and human wills. Rules of all descriptions are always simultaneously social constructions and resources for the ongoing cycle of social construction.

Before analyzing the relationship between these rule types and their role in the constitution of international society, we must briefly attend to the nature and character of *jus cogens* in international law. As set out in Articles 53 and 64 of the 1969 *Vienna Convention on the Law of Treaties,* norms of this character admit of no exceptions. Any treaty—and by extrapolation, any act—in contravention of such a norm is always automatically wrong and by consequence void. Such obligations cannot be contracted out of *inter se.* Their violation neither is nor can ever be allowable; neither can violation ever be excusable.[8]

Jus cogens are the rules that are uppermost in the hierarchy of a society's norms; historically, this function was fulfilled by the rules of Natural Law. A *legitimate* violation of Natural Law was not only unthinkable, it was by definition impossible in the same way that a violation of the physical laws of nature was understood to be materially impossible. Indeed, the categorical character of *jus cogens* imparts an uncomfortable Natural Law flavor, which seems to be at the base of much of the explanatory difficulty surrounding the concept. This will be addressed in Chapter 3. Although *jus cogens* were formulated in Positivist terms in the Vienna Convention, and have their root in Roman law, their apparent Natural Law character requires a different approach to understanding the basis of their normativity. We construct normative hierarchies in ways that reflect our *values*. Some values and the norms deriving from them are always special. Some are considered particularly important because they are necessary for the very functioning of the rest of the normative system, and hence foundational (the norms *pacta sunt servanda* and *rebus sic stantibus* in international law).[9] Others because they reflect our widely and deeply held moral sentiments about what it means to be who we are (the categorical bans on slavery and genocide), and are thus uppermost among the hierarchy of norms.

I do not, however, want to equate *jus cogens* with morality *simpliciter;* peremptory norms may reflect or embody morality or sentiments (one would be hard-pressed to find any high-level principles of law that do not), but they are in the first instance part of Positive Law. The peremptory, categorical character and bindingness of these laws have a moral basis. It is for moral reasons that we have *made* them exceptionless; it is for moral reasons that we have *endowed* them with peremptory standing. *Jus cogens* rules are "more binding" than other rules of *jus disposituvum* character because, in our moral vocabulary, we cannot conceive of legitimate grounds for their violation whatever the circumstances. Consequently, neither can we countenance any circumstances precluding the wrongfulness of their violation.[10]

The rules having *jus cogens* character in any society play a more fundamental role in defining that society than other primary rules by making certain foundational stipulations such as "These are the things we unconditionally prohibit" and "These are the things we unconditionally require." In reality, these obligations are not purely unconditional because all norms, including peremptory norms, change. As indicated previously, this is a signal point of differentiation from Natural Law. Although Article 53 of the Vienna Convention acknowledges that a *jus cogens* rule can be supplanted, it limits this possibility to replacement by another norm of the same character.

This caveat notwithstanding, the function of rules of *jus cogens* character is to indicate that if an agent violates them or rejects their unconditionality, that party excludes itself thereby from membership in this society.

The body of rules to which a society ascribes peremptory standing is constituted by what Richard Rorty has called its "final vocabulary." "All human beings carry about a set of words which they employ to justify their actions, their beliefs, and their lives . . . [I] call these words a person's 'final vocabulary.'"[11] Rorty employs the Aristotelian-sounding language of finality because such a vocabulary is final in the sense that if it is challenged, its user has no way to argue on its behalf but to employ terms taken from the vocabulary itself; it cannot be defended noncircularly. It is, Rorty says, as far as the user can go with language. Beyond these words "is only helpless passivity or a resort to force." In performing this function, the final vocabulary is the means by which the society articulates (however contingently in the eyes of an observer or properly ironic society member) its bedrock beliefs and sentiments such as "These are the beliefs we hold unconditionally, the beliefs that make us who we are." It provides the means by which the society determines the things it unconditionally prohibits or requires, condemns or lauds. Like parties disclaiming rules of *jus cogens,* parties who do not hold these beliefs are not part of the relevant "us" or "we." If "they" do not share in what "we" consider (however contingently) defines "us," they cannot be "us."

A society's secondary rules specify the means by which any norm can become enshrined in the Positive (primary) Law of that society; they detail as well how the status of existing laws can be changed from dispositive to peremptory. The legitimacy of any primary rule candidate—especially one claiming peremptory status—is determined by a set of antecedent secondary rules, but despite secondary rules being in this regard logically prior to (peremptory) primary rules, other *jus cogens* rules also play a role in the ongoing process of constitution. These rules are a factor in setting the very criteria by which agents use secondary rules to evaluate primary rule candidates, and indeed in setting out the secondary rules themselves—hence the analogy to Kelsen's *Grundnorm.*

The overall relationship of final vocabulary, *jus cogens,* and international society is recursive and circular; no one element can be changed without having an effect on the others. In the apparently simple case, when our final vocabulary changes, it results in a change in the body of (simple) primary and *jus cogens* primary rules; this results in a change in the character of the international society. This change in final vocabulary may, depending on the subject matter, also exert an influence on the secondary rules themselves; we may, for example, come to view our rules of recognition as too narrow and exclusionary, and call for their revision.

Changes of final vocabulary do not arise *ex nihilo;* they often arise from the dynamics of the very society they constitute. Although institutionalization may serve to strengthen the hold of our final vocabulary, other factors (including especially the unintended consequences of institutionalization) may come into play, and these may make some of "us" question "our" final vocabulary, attempt its replacement, and begin the cycle anew.

Calls to restructure the current international society are, in fact, manifestations of either changes in "our" final vocabulary or perhaps the emergence of a new, incommensurable final vocabulary exerting new demands and expressing new valuations. Besides critique from within, another way this change may take place is by the addition (constitution) of new agents. The rules establishing the means by which agency is gained are themselves a subset of the secondary rules constituting the international society. For example, with the advent of decolonization (itself the effect of previous changes in international society), new voices making new and unfamiliar demands were heard. As some of these demands were gradually accepted and became internalized by the society that these "new" states had joined, the final vocabulary of international society changed, international society's *jus cogens* changed, and finally, international society itself changed. International society was in this regard reconstituted by the inclusion of new agents. More often, of course, these demands were repressed and there was no change, but the intervention into the cycle of co-constitution by agents who had not participated in previous iterations of the cycle and who brought with them new and potentially revolutionary values and demands remains a potential source for change.

Plan of the Book

To show how this process may work, the rest of this book addresses the story of the rise, fall, and rise again of the practice of international punishment. Generically, punishment connotes the use of force against a party that has committed a wrong by another party whether or not the second party was specifically injured by the first. Domestically, the state punishes criminals even though it is often private individuals who are the materially injured parties. Often this concept implies a relation of authority, punisher over punished. By contrast, retaliation is the standard instrument of self-help in Realist understandings of international relations (IR), where in the absence of a supranational authority, one state responds in kind to an injury inflicted by another state.

Although Realists characterize IR as having essentially always been a self-help system, punishment was also the norm in the sixteenth and seventeenth centuries. Starting with Grotius and his antecedents in Chapter 2, we will see the development, demise, and potential rebirth of an international system in which actors (not only states) could use force against any other party should there be a violation of any of the fundamental rules of the system. As detailed most famously by Richard Tuck, it was a commonplace between the sixteenth and nineteenth centuries that nations and later states had the right to use force to punish other states for violating certain of international society's rules, without regard to whether the punishing state or its nationals had been affected by the violations—in other words, without regard to legal standing. Every nation / state had this right; in principle, any nation / state anywhere could punish any other nation / state for any violation of Natural Law.

This practice arose in a period when sovereignty as both principle and practice remained inchoate. Likewise, international punishment was conceptualized in Natural Law terms; the rules binding nations / states had sources independent of human (or nation / state) will, and need never have been accepted by any nation / state. Nations, like individual persons, were simply bound by certain universal rules. As the meaning of sovereignty evolved toward our current understanding, especially in its emphasis on Voluntarism, and its being a property of *states,* the practice of international punishment became conceptually unsustainable, and was largely set aside.[12] In the older scenario, neither authority nor injury nor standing were predicates to punishment; the mere violation of the rule was sufficient to give *any* other party the standing to punish the offender. There are many noteworthy elements to this largely Grotian vision, to be worked out in the next chapter, but what is central at the moment is that the rules in question were the Laws of Nature, exogenous to the will of those bound by them, and the subjects of these laws were not states *per se,* but nations.

The differentiation between state and nation (and the parallel differentiation between both of those terms and sovereign) is part of what caused international punishment to fall out of favor. Nations as congeries of natural persons were regarded as bound by Natural Law; states as artificial persons distinct from the natural persons they "personated" were progressively harder to portray as bound by Natural Law.[13] As long as sovereigns were discrete individuals, they could be considered bound by Natural Law, but when the transition to the idea of the state itself being sovereign was effected, Natural Law as a system of rules imposed by a nonhuman source grew increasingly difficult to defend. The sovereign, artificial person of the state was bound only by voluntarily agreed-to Positive Laws, and was bound by them only so long as it continued to assent. Most importantly, as sovereign, these artificial persons (states) were considered the juridical equals of one another, and not subject to the judgment of one another. In the absence of judgment, of course, there could no longer be punishment. What remained, as we will see in Chapter 2, was reprisal.

The practice of international punishment, as Chapter 2 will show, went through a series of transformations before eventually being rejected. These transformations, and the ultimate rejection of the legitimacy of punishment in international society—representing fundamental shifts in the secondary and *jus cogens* rules—correlate very closely with the rise of Positivism in law, the displacement of Natural Law, and the concomitant move toward a more rigid conception of sovereignty and the sovereign equality of states. Each of these conceptual and political changes made punishment progressively more difficult to justify, because each undermined one of the pillars justifying the practice. However, subsequent changes in the last 60 years have opened the door to new manifestations of discrete aspects of international punishment, but in ways rooted in a different normative framework. The remainder of this book details how individual component practices have reemerged to produce a new, still inchoate, form of international punishment as our understanding of sovereignty has again been reconfigured. Each of the remaining chapters of this book will address how portions of the old practice have come back in new form—the new form is not predicated upon the use of military force, however; it keeps punishment wholly within the realm of legal practices.[14]

As we have seen telegraphically already, there were three main components to classical international punishment: absolutely and universally binding nonconsensual rules, universal standing to punish those who violate the rules without regard to injury or interest, and an understanding of sovereignty without implications of inviolability or the sort of immunity from judgment that comes from juridical equality. Chapters 3 through 6 will each address developments in international law and international politics that seem to indicate a return to the punitive ethos characteristic of the late Renaissance and early modern period.

Somewhat paradoxically, considering the key explanatory role that *jus cogens* plays here, the subject matter of Chapter 3 is *jus cogens* itself. There is obviously a certain amount of circularity—if not question begging—in using the concept of *jus cogens* to explain the workings of *jus cogens*. But it is important to recognize that in the period of Positivist Voluntarism's greatest dominance, the concept of norms peremptory to all others disappeared from international law, even if in practical terms the sovereignty-Positivism normative complex was treated as outweighing other norms. The very introduction of *jus cogens* into the discourse of international law represented a fundamental change in the body of *jus cogens* rules of international society.

There is nothing *per se* punitive about *jus cogens;* indeed, the majority of rules of all characters are not directly concerned with punishment. The fact remains, however, that one of the pillars of international punishment has returned, albeit in attenuated form. The larger purpose of Chapter 3 will be to explain how we can conceptualize categorical obligation in a still predominantly Voluntarist setting. On its face, these two notions are all but antithetical; can an obligation be both indefeasible and voluntary? How can a rule of Positive Law be as absolute and exceptionless as a rule of the Law of Nature?

The first pillar of international punishment was absolute rules of universal scope. The second—logically dependent upon the first—was the universal standing to enforce those rules. This pillar also tumbled under challenge from Positivist Voluntarism. Modern international law has conceptualized obligations as bilateral in character even when the instruments declaring them were multilateral in scope. International law does not generally understand obligations to be owed to the community of states at large. Standing to seek redress for the violation of a rule was (and remains) overwhelmingly limited only to parties directly and materially injured by the violation. There was nothing necessary about this: bilateral agreements were simply more common historically, and bilateral obligation was the cognitive framework within which early multilateral agreements were formulated, and this conceptualization has been utilized ever since.

As we will see in Chapter 4, the last few decades have seen the enunciation—if not clear-cut application—of a new manifestation (admittedly with hesitation) of the second pillar. Since the 1970s, international law has recognized the existence of obligations *erga omnes,* obligations that are owed to the international community generally. Some have postulated that violation of these obligations, since they are owed to the international community generally, gives rise to general standing to enforce them, namely, to the *actio popularis.* Based on a practice from Roman law, the *actio popularis* is an action brought against a malfeasant not on the personal behalf of the party bringing the action (nor like a criminal action is it brought by the state), but on behalf of the community. In international law, it is one state making a legal claim against another not for an injury it suffered by the conduct of the latter, but for the latter's mere violation of an obligation owed generally (an obligation *erga omnes*). This practice is well known in many domestic legal settings, but it has been greeted simultaneously with trepidation and skepticism in international law.

The emphasis with obligations *erga omnes* is not on violations of Natural Law punishable by any and all, but rather positive, voluntarily undertaken obligations to *all* legally actionable by *any*. In principle, every state has a legal interest in the observance of obligations *erga omnes;* thus, any state (it has been asserted) may take legal action to ensure compliance with an obligation *erga omnes*. This is a more obvious manifestation of international punishment than *jus cogens,* but both practices are related, and part of the purpose of Chapter 4 will be to sort out that relationship and to moderate the enthusiastic equation of the two. Do peremptory norms *eo ipso* create obligations that bind all relevant agents? Does the mere violation of a *jus cogens* rule create universal standing to enforce? Conversely, this chapter will address the question of whether universally binding obligations are necessarily categorical.

The issues addressed in chapters 3 and 4 deal primarily with the return of international punishment's jurisdictional features. Introducing (or reintroducing) them to international law brought back the classical idea of rules not necessarily voluntarily undertaken that create obligations to the international community as a whole and that can in principle be enforced—albeit only by litigation—by any member of that society. Those chapters examine interstate obligations, but by traveling between levels of analysis, Chapter 5 allows us to see a manifestation of international punishment that is more plainly recognizable as descended from the older practice. In Chapter 5, we look at internationalized *individual* legal obligation and the circumstances under which violation of laws directly binding individuals might give rise to international responsibility and the *general standing to prosecute.* The issues of chapters 3 and 4 represent manifestations of the resurgence of the idea of universally enforceable rules; in those cases, the obligations are held by states, and their violation is not generally treated as criminal (however, see the discussion in Chapter 6 *infra* of state criminality). Chapter 5 introduces another major change in the fundamental rules of international society; this change is starkest when seen in light of the conflict between universal jurisdiction over international crimes and sovereign (head of state) immunity. There has been tremendous development in the idea of universal jurisdiction since the end of World War Two, but the roots go back much further. Notwithstanding some tenuous prefigurations to be found as far back as Justinian's *Codex* (534 CE), the right of any state to try and to punish pirates as enemies of humanity (*hostes humani generis*) provides the model for modern prosecution and punishment of international criminals. Rather than a *new* manifestation of international punishment, this may be one that has existed all along, but it is clear that the scope of universal jurisdiction has changed—the classes of persons over whom universal jurisdiction may be exercised has expanded, as has the range of crimes.

As with classical international punishment, we find a system in which standing to prosecute and punish is independent of direct injury or other material link to the crime. The Principle of Universal Jurisdiction (sometimes rendered the Universality Principle) gives all states the right to prosecute individuals who have been accused of committing any of a specified set of international crimes. Rather than offering a general account of international criminal law, the purpose of Chapter 5 is to trace the development of this specific jurisdictional principle from its antecedents to recent questions about the relationship between jurisdiction over universally prohibited and criminalized acts on the one hand and sovereign immunity / head of state immunity on the other.

The development of universal jurisdiction brings another aspect of punishment back into the picture. In the classical formulation, any violation of one of international society's highest norms could be punished by anyone. This was eventually replaced by the opposite belief (and practice) that no violation could be punished by anyone. The year 1945 ushered in (or at least solidified) the idea of international crime. International crimes were conceptualized as crimes that can have been committed anywhere and can be prosecuted and punished by any state without regard to whether that state, or its nationals, is an injured party; these are crimes not only against the material victims, but also against international society at large. These are crimes *erga omnes.* In 1945, it was the allies who took responsibility for these punishments, but they did so on behalf of the Nazi's victims as well as for injuries done to their own states and nationals. This was classic international punishment in one sense, allowing judgment and punishment without regard to specific legal interest or standing, but it differed fundamentally from Grotius's formulation in two important ways: it was based on Positive Law, and there was a very explicit shift toward individual responsibility and away from collective liability.

Chapters 3 through 5 each focus on the rehabilitation of a particular pillar of international punishment; Chapter 6 confronts current efforts to revive the old practice in its entirety. In it, we turn to recent efforts to criminalize the acts of states, to conceptualize states as criminals, and to articulate modes of punishing states. This is a particularly troubling venture, because like the classical practice of international punishment, the means of punishment is the use of force in many instances, although in some accounts sanctions fall under this heading as well.

These efforts are misguided for multiple reasons. There are theoretical problems with the underlying notions of state agency and state action that rely on metaphors of state personhood that cannot bear the conceptual burden. Chapter 6's argument against the idea that states can commit crimes and thus against the punishment of states rests on the requirement in most legal systems that for a person to commit most crimes they must possess the requisite intent. Intent requires a mind. Although it is certainly commonplace to speak of states having interests, deliberating, and acting, this is, of course, figurative language. It rests on the Hobbesian (or Hobbespopularized) metaphor of the state as person; in unpacking this metaphor, I destabilize each of the predicate elements necessary to assert that states can commit crimes. There are larger and more damning moral problems with holding whole populations responsible for the acts of discrete individuals. More than previous chapters, Chapter 6 has an explicitly normative, in addition to an analytic, purpose, challenging ideas of collective responsibility and collective guilt that have become ever more commonplace.

CHAPTER 2

The Historical Trajectory of International Punishment

As was briefly alluded to in the preceding chapter, Realist IR theorists have tended to characterize IR as having essentially always been a self-help system in which states use force to promote, defend, or vindicate their own interests; we need not read it as always having been that way. Alongside the self-interested, self-help ethos and its attendant practices, a punitive ethos operated for a period of centuries. Unlike the self-help regime—and it is indeed a congeries of *rules*—that requires only more-or-less like units in interaction, the punitive ethos was predicated upon a very specific legal-normative context. The practice, however, went through a series of transformations before eventually being rejected. International punishment, as both idea and practice, evolved in a context unlike that of the current international system, and as we will see in the coming sections, each move from that context toward our own undermined the legitimacy of invoking punishment as a grounds for the just use of force. International punishment was rooted in and legitimated by a particular understanding of sovereignty and by specific understandings of the source and character of obligation; in their absence, punishment could no longer serve to satisfy the *jus ad bellum* criterion of "just cause." The contingent products of a unique intellectual setting, as these understandings were superseded, international punishment lost its coherence and became indefensible.

These transformations, and the ultimate rejection of the legitimacy of punishment in international society—representing fundamental shifts in the secondary rules and *jus cogens* primary rules—correlate very closely with the rise of Positivism in law, the displacement of Natural Law, and the parallel but related move toward a more rigid conception of sovereignty and the sovereign equality of states. Each of these conceptual and political changes made international punishment progressively more difficult to defend, because they each undermined one of the pillars justifying the practice. However, changes in the last 65 years have opened the door to new manifestations of aspects of international punishment, but in ways rooted in a different normative framework.

This story cannot be told without devoting careful attention to sovereignty as both concept and practice. Nonetheless, there is no need for another history, deconstruction, or genealogy of sovereignty.[1] Although this story depends upon analyzing some of the changes to the earlier absolute ideas of sovereignty, there is no need for another premature announcement of sovereignty's demise.

Punishment and sovereignty are mutually dependent terms in much the same way that Cynthia Weber demonstrated the co-constitution of intervention and sovereignty.[2] Classical international punishment was only able to take the form it did because of a still inchoate conception (and practice) of sovereignty; as the idea and related practices became more formalized, institutionalized, ritualized, and internalized, punishment became theoretically insupportable and politically unpalatable. Conversely "sovereign" came to be identified as what is subject to neither external judgment nor punishment. Punishment's replacement—reprisal—differed only in its justification. In the place of punishment, reprisal, which is tied closely to self-help, and had operated alongside punishment, came to the fore, but it has also largely fallen from favor both doctrinally and in practice. Punishment connotes relations of authority and subordination; reprisal is suited precisely to interactions among juridical equals—perhaps because it was originally a practice involving individuals and what we would currently call nonstate actors. The remainder of the book after this chapter details the new shapes that international punishment has taken; the purpose of this chapter—in addition to explaining the fall from use of international punishment—is to show the changes in our conceptualization of sovereignty that have made these new manifestations possible.

Debating Punishment

"Justifiable causes [of war] include defense, the obtaining of that which belongs to us or is our due, and *the infliction of punishment*."[3]

Borrowing heavily from classical Roman jurisprudence, Hugo Grotius asserted that any violation of Natural Law entailed a right to punish.[4] There was no question of standing, interest, or injury; any nation had the right to punish any violator of the Laws of Nature.[5]

> Kings and those who are invested with a power equal to that of Kings, have a right to exact punishments, not only for injuries committed against themselves, or their subjects, but likewise, for those which do not peculiarly concern them, but which are, in any persons whatsoever, grievous violations of the Law of Nature or Nations. For the liberty of consulting the benefit of human society, by punishments, which at first . . . was in every particular person, does now, since civil societies, and courts of justice, have been instituted, reside in those who are possessed of the supreme power.[6]

The prohibitions against *inter alia* cannibalism and attacking peaceful settlers were *jus cogens* even if this epithet was not employed; such acts were violations of the Law of Nature, and the prohibitions against them were peremptory by definition. As stated in the previous chapter, a *legitimate* violation of Natural Law was not merely unthinkable; it was a definitional and logical impossibility.[7]

In Grotius's account, there was a universal right for any nation to punish any violator of the Natural Law. "Grotius effectively recasts natural law precepts in terms of rights and correlative duties by calling upon the Roman law conception of cause of action and remedy."[8] Punishing violators of the Law of Nature was a right *erga omnes;* the right of punishment was predicated upon the prohibition against these proscribed acts being an obligation *erga omnes*. If Natural Law prohibited an act, the obligation not to commit that act was owed by all and owed *to* all. Because the obligation was owed to every other member of international society, each of them had an interest in seeing the obligation met, and had a resulting right to either ensure that it was met or mete out punishment for its violation.

Grotius asserted a right for nations (and, in fact, private corporations) to punish parties over whom they had no political or legal authority; a nation's right to punish a violator of the Natural Law stemmed from the individual's antecedent right to punish violators of the Natural Law in the State of Nature.[9] In the State of Nature, in our presocial condition, punishment was necessarily carried out by men (and in Grotius it *was* men) who did not—and definitionally could not—possess authority over those whom they punished, but it is a requirement of Natural Law that "Evil deeds must be corrected."[10] There was by definition no sovereign to enforce the law, but allowing violations of Natural Law was intolerable; therefore, Grotius concluded that the power to "correct" must have been held by all persons equally.[11] This power must also have been held not just by the injured, but was "a right vested in *every* inhabitant of the state of nature."[12] As Benjamin Straumann carefully notes, there is no necessary criminality to the violation of Natural Law, but punishment is still to be issued. "The right to punish arises out of a wrong. Since for Grotius such a wrong can—true to his Roman law terminology—be both a simple private delict and a behavior that is criminally relevant."[13]

Grotius "simply" translated this into the nation's identical right, because for him there were no important conceptual distinctions between individuals in the State of Nature and nations; nations had no powers that individuals had not had in the State of Nature. Individuals had transferred their right to punish upon the creation of society, and as Ulpian noted in D.50.17.54, "No one can transfer greater rights to someone else than he possesses himself."[14] This entails the rights to both return any wrong done to oneself (reprisal) and avenge any wrong—entailing a violation of the Law of Nature—done to *anyone* (punishment).[15] Grotius argued that in the State of Nature (and hence in IR) there is what we, borrowing from Roman law, call an *actio popularis,* or what he (following Seneca) called the *right of the private avenger.*[16] "Translated to a world where commonwealths have come into existence, the natural right to punish entitles every sovereign to punish severe violations of the legal order, even if neither the sovereign himself nor the citizens within his jurisdiction have been injured by the violation in question."[17] This becomes one of the cornerstones of Grotius's thought on *jus ad bellum,* and sets the stage for discussion of just causes for war during the following two and a half centuries.

The amenability of Grotius's position to European imperialism is obvious and well known: if you are cannibals, force may be used to punish you. If you kill people who come to settle on your "unused" land, force may be used against you.[18] If you do not allow people to settle on your "unused" land as the Law of Nature says that you must, force may be used against you. If you refuse to allow people (us) to trade with you as the Law of Nature says that you must, force may be used against you. If you refuse to allow passage through the seas, force may be used against you. Punishment might likewise be inflicted for "offenses against God," but not merely for rejecting Christianity, and for conducting human sacrifices.[19]

Under then contemporary understandings of the *jus ad bellum,* the infliction of punishment was considered to be a just cause for the use of force. Of course, the idea predated Grotius, and he was careful to demonstrate the classical roots of this understanding in *inter alia* Cicero and Augustine. His contribution was unique, however, in a number of respects. The classical authors tended to use the term in a more narrow sense with implications closer to reprisal (a requirement of prior injury to the punishing party), and as has been noted, Grotius asserted that the right was still held by private parties as well as nations.[20] In his understanding of what would come to be called the social contract, individuals had transmitted their right to punish to nations upon their creation, but had not done so *exclusively* or *exhaustively.* For Grotius, in other words, individuals apparently retained the natural right to punish, but not the political right to exercise the right to punish; they were, therefore, able to transfer or delegate it a second time to non-state actors. In this understanding, the authority in question in the *jus ad bellum* formulation of "right authority" was always derivative of our original natural rights.

What is important theoretically about Grotius's position is that besides the existence of a generalized right of punishment, the locus of punishment was not understood to be the political abstraction we call the state; it might be individuals, as was the case with the "punishment" carried out by Dutch privateers, or it might be an entire society. In practice, punishment might entail conquest and subjugation of the entire nation.[21] Although individuals were the material perpetrators of crimes, the public at large bore collective responsibility for them, presumably because either they were collectively complicit, themselves guilty of the same crimes at other times, or the instant perpetrators were unidentifiable. Conversely, liability could flow upward as well; Grotius insisted that "a nation and its magistrates incur guilt when they fail to curb the openly shameful conduct of their people."[22] He started with the individual responsibility of the ruler, but very quickly slid over to the punishment of the community at large. He first asserted that the whole will not be responsible for the acts of individuals unless they concur, but offered an expansive understanding of "concur" that only required having knowledge of a crime and not preventing it. He did qualify the stringency of this position by making the power to prevent the crime a precondition of responsibility, but then immediately vitiated this by insisting that the public will know of the acts of those who rule them.[23] "It is universally admitted that acts which have taken place because of the nation's decision, and even those which have been decreed by a major part of the whole nation or by magistrates, are acts of the whole community . . . the subjects of a state that is shown to have inflicted an injury are liable, as such, to warlike attack."[24]

An important predicate of Grotius's theory was that it contained no notion of the state as an entity *sui generis* separate from the ruler and the populace that bore rights and responsibilities. Grotius was able to make the claims he did, in part, because he did not yet have a notion of state sovereignty entailing immunity from outside scrutiny or sanction such as we later find in Positivism. This is not to say that he altogether lacked a notion of sovereignty. Setting aside the question of the fidelity of treating *summum imperium, summum potestatem,* and *regnatrice imperium* as Latin equivalents of "sovereignty," nearly his entire discussion of what later translators render as "sovereignty" is focused domestically.[25] That said, there is a rather mystifying passage at I.II.VI.2 and .3 of *De Jure Belli* in which—if we read him in Aristotelian terms—he might be construed as asserting that the state (bearing in mind my previous caveat) is sovereign.

> The subject of power is either common or special. Just as the body is a common, the eye a special subject of the power of sight, so the state (*civitas*) . . . is the common subject of sovereignty (*summae potestatis*). It may be granted that the common subject of sovereignty (*summae potestatis*) is the state (*civitas*) . . . The special subject is one or more persons according to the laws and customs of each nation (*gentium*).

Julius Goebel asserts, "Grotius conceived of the subjects of the law of nations as being completely independent of the political control and consequently of the will of each other."[26] This is hard to reconcile with their authority to punish one another, unless either Grotius had a radically different (or incomplete) conception of the term or one subscribes to his inversion of the punishment relationship; many of his critics did not.

The first significant criticism of Grotius's views on international punishment came from Samuel Pufendorf, who was fundamentally averse to Grotius's claim that one state can punish another for violating Natural Law. This was, in part, the result of Pufendorf's skepticism about punishment being a right held by individuals in the State of Nature. In his understanding, in the State of Nature we could at most retaliate for a wrong done to us.[27] On the contrary, for Pufendorf (following Thomas Hobbes) punishment is by its very definition administered by a superior, by one who has legal or political *authority* over the perpetrator. This requires established laws recognized by the subjects and enforced by a sovereign, but definitionally (and here Pufendorf hews closely to Hobbes), there were neither laws nor sovereigns in the State of Nature; therefore, there could be no punishment in the State of Nature, only retaliation.[28] Of course, this points to a larger disagreement with Grotius, for whom we are already fully rule bound in the State of Nature by the Laws of Nature. By contrast, Pufendorf took a line much closer to that of Hobbes, positing that Natural Law was a minimal code for coexistence. Pufendorf was willing to countenance the use of force against a state that has not harmed another only in the particular circumstance of intervention at the request of people suffering "insupportable Tyranny and Cruelties," but this is conceptually distinct from punishment, and more akin to modern ideas of humanitarian intervention.[29]

Pufendorf's challenge was answered by John Locke in the *Second Treatise* and in the "Essays on the Law of Nature," which offered what amounted to restatements of Grotius's position.[30] Locke's position is Grotian, as is his argument; he states in the *Second Treatise* what he himself describes as what "will seem a very strange Doctrine":

> All Men may be restrained from invading others Rights, and from doing hurt to one another, and the Law of Nature be observed, which willeth the Peace and *Preservation of all Mankind,* the *Execution* of the Law of Nature is in that State, put into every Mans hands, whereby every one has a right to punish the transgressors of that Law to such a Degree as may hinder its Violation. For the *Law of Nature* would . . . be in vain, if there were no body that in the State of Nature had a *Power to Execute* that Law, and thereby preserve the innocent and restrain offenders, and if anyone in the State of Nature may punish another . . . everyone may do so . . . what any may do in Prosecution of that Law, everyone must needs have a right to do.[31]

> In transgressing the Law of Nature, the offender . . . becomes dangerous to Mankind . . . [the offense] being a trespass against the whole Species, and the Peace and Safety of [the Species] . . . every man . . . may restrain, or where it is necessary destroy things noxious to them, and so may bring such evil on anyone, who hath transgressed that Law . . . And in this case, and upon this ground, *every Man hath a Right to punish the Offender, and be Executioner of the Law of Nature.*[32]

At least Locke's leap of reasoning in moving from the State of Nature to sovereign rights in IR is more apparent if no more compelling: he asserted rightly that a sovereign may exercise authority over a visiting foreigner, but when he then slid directly from there to a purported corollary right to punish persons for crimes against nature that they commit in their own lands, he returned to familiar Grotian argumentation. However, as Alex Tuckness has noted, Locke has a stricter standard for determining who in the political community shares in the state's misconduct.[33]

Significant challenges to the Grotian / Lockean punitive model were signaled by the work of G. W. Leibniz, Christian Wolff, and Emer Vattel. Although we have already discussed the vexed passage from Grotius arguably attributing sovereignty to states, it is more definitive that since Leibniz, sovereignty has come to be regarded as an attribute of the state. The focus since Leibniz has been upon freedom of action and freedom from interference. Leibniz was motivated by the disunity of Germany, nominally under the authority of the Holy Roman Empire (labeled by Leibniz's adversary Pufendorf, a "monster"), and the relations between the various principalities that comprised it. Existing diplomatic practice as well as some contemporary conceptualizations of sovereignty left some of the principalities "un-sovereign," while others were considered to be sovereign. Leibniz was faced with a paradox: how to make sovereignty compatible with the allegiance a lesser state "might owe a universal power"?

From this starting point, Leibniz set out to reconceptualize sovereignty. Torbjørn Knutsen identified three conditions operative in Leibniz's account: minimum size, *majestas,* and actual control over territory.[34] The first and third were those of practical concern, whereas *majestas* seems more backward looking—it evoked the Roman legal tradition and the influence that tradition had upon the medieval world.[35] Ironically, in *Caeserinus Fürstenerius,* Leibniz's most important work on the topic, he castigates others "who undertake to write [on sovereignty] have eyes only for what is ancient, [and] of which vestiges scarcely survive, while they are not interested in more modern things."[36]

For Leibniz, territory, Knutsen's first requisite, is both the physical space as well as the "aggregate of laws and rights" in force there. From this Leibniz deduced the concept of "territorial hegemony." Territorial hegemony entails jurisdiction and authority, and is bolstered by *majestas;* two other central factors are the power of coercion (common as well to Bodin and Hobbes) and the right of military might. Coercion is the simple power to use force on "stubborn people"; the right of military might is of far greater importance. It represents both dominance over the stubborn within and the ability and right to keep "the whole dominion in its duty." Leibniz's territorial hegemony is thus the highest right of coercing. It is here that the ostensibly nonsovereign principalities are the equals of others not nominally subject to the empire. "Sovereign is he who is master of a territory and who is powerful enough to make himself considerable in Europe in time of peace and in time of war, by treaties, arms and alliances."[37] In fact, a state may give away many rights *(regalia)* without in any way jeopardizing its sovereignty.[38] All that matters is that "he have in readiness the power to obtain from his subjects, either by his dignity, or, when necessary, by *force majeure,* whatever rights do remain his."[39] These *regalia* are merely ornamentation upon the heart of sovereignty, the ability to enforce a state's independent existence.

> Those persons only are called sovereigns or potentates who hold a large territory and can lead out an army. And this it is, finally, which I call supremacy . . . those larger powers which can wage war, sustain it, survive somehow by their own power, make treaties, take part with authority in the affairs of other peoples: [in short], powers which are somehow exempt from the commerce of private persons and which, as human affairs now stand, cannot easily fall to lower person, or persons of lesser standing. [40]

As Knutsen aptly puts it, the *sine qua non* of sovereignty is the ability to control one's subjects without being likewise subject to the control of a superior power.[41] It does not matter if the sovereign "holds his lands as a fief, nor whether he recognizes the majesty of a chief, provided that he be master at home and cannot be disturbed except by arms."[42] The internal aspects of sovereignty focused upon by Bodin and Hobbes were thus put into an international context. Not only could there be only one sovereign within a commonwealth, but that sovereign must be immune from control from without; as such, however, that state would be the *legal* equal of all others.[43]

Christian Wolff is traditionally treated as squarely within the Natural Law tradition, but a close reading will show that, despite extensive discussion and ritual obeisance,[44] he downplays the role of Natural Law at every opportunity in favor of Positive Law.[45] This move in Wolff away from Natural Law is conjoined with a stronger articulation of sovereignty than had been found in Grotius, or indeed Pufendorf, because he built upon Leibniz's ideas. Interestingly, even in his articulation of Natural Law, he emphasized rules that generated a very strong notion of state sovereignty and the sovereign equality of states, which entailed that all states have freedom of action that may not be limited by others.[46] We can see in this the continuation of Leibniz's conceptual efforts to externalize sovereignty, and to turn it into a property or attribute of the state that characterizes its relations with other states.

Wolff sided generally with Pufendorf on the matter of international punishment, if not through a line of argument that Pufendorf would have found agreeable. Wolff's starting point was the notional international community he called the *Civitas Maxima;* this state of states is possessed, Wolff claimed, of a "limited sovereignty" over its component member states,[47] but presaging later developments, he stressed that it is a community of equal members.[48] This led him to allow the international community (but deny its individual member states) a highly circumscribed right to police the conduct of any state.[49] He then pushed even beyond Pufendorf in prohibiting *any* sort of intervention, no matter how terrible the abuse or tyranny. No matter how terrible the abuse or tyranny, no state, no collection of states has any right to judge the conduct of another state in its domestic affairs.[50] The sole vestige of allowable punishment or intervention Wolff retained was war against states that fight war for its own sake.[51]

Vattel, although he is often dismissed as a mere popularizer of Wolff, built significantly upon the latter's ideas, and in many instances disagreed with Wolff outright, most notably with regard to the idea of the *Civitas Maxima.*[52] Vattel built well beyond Wolff's conception of sovereignty, offering an even stronger account, including especially the right of every state to "govern itself as it thinks proper, and that no one of them has the least right to interfere in the government of another."[53] Vattel parted with Wolff in supporting the right to intervene on behalf of oppressed peoples who have requested assistance. This put him (in this regard) closer to Pufendorf than to Wolff, but even here, note the continued shift toward intervention and away from punishment. Despite having made allowance for humanitarian intervention, the use of force on behalf of the people against their rulers, he did not believe that liability could flow in the opposite direction—the people collectively could not be responsible for the acts of their rulers, or even their fellows.

> It is impossible for the best governed state or the most watchful and strict sovereign to regulate at will all the acts of their subjects . . . it would be unjust to impute to the Nation or the sovereign, all the faults of their citizens. Hence it cannot be asserted in general that one has been injured by a Nation because one has been injured by one of its citizens.[54]

Considering this, Vattel remained adamantly against the position still associated with Grotius.

It is really Vattel whose thought represents the fundamental changes from Grotius to the beliefs and practices dominant through 1945. Vattel, much more strongly than Wolff, provided a rigid formulation of sovereignty; he also further (and drastically so) diminished the role of Natural Law and increased the role of Positive Law.[55] In Vattel's work, Natural Law was considered only hortatory in function and weight. Natural law was no longer *enforceable* at all. For Vattel, all obligation—all meaningful obligation—was voluntary, and as such, only the violation of these obligations was liable of sanction. Of equal importance, sanction could only be sought or imposed by an injured party. The *actio popularis,* the last of the foundations of the right of punishment, had now vanished from international law altogether. The significance of this change in the rules and character of international society can hardly be overstated.

The Abandonment of International Punishment

For the next two centuries, the *Absolute Sovereignty–Voluntarism–Positivism Complex* dictated the fundamental rules of international society. Under these rules, no state might legitimately interfere in the domestic affairs of another, states were not subject to any obligation they had not voluntarily undertaken, states might not be coerced into fulfilling their obligations, and there was no hierarchy among norms or obligations. By comparison, the fundamental rules of international society during the period from Grotius to Vattel were a complex of *Inchoate Sovereignty, Adjurationism,* and *Naturalism.* In this latter rule complex, sovereignty was not considered indefeasible (nor was it necessarily associated with the nation / state); obligation was not limited to voluntary acceptance, and was understood to be amenable to external imposition; and Natural Law was considered to outweigh any positive obligation, whether stemming from treaty or state practice (customary international law). It was this constellation of fundamental rules that allowed for international punishment; change any and the claim to justly punish another state is that much weaker; change all three in the directions that were taken, and international punishment becomes no longer justifiable at all.

Bear in mind, however, that not all states were at all times regarded as equal members of this society, and those on the outside were not afforded this respect or these protections. Gerry Simpson offers a compelling characterization that is in many ways at odds with that just presented. For Simpson, the period properly characterized by the former normative complex ended not in 1945, but in 1815, with the emergence of new forms of hierarchy in the international system.[56] Nonetheless, the linguistic and ideational framing in which punishment *qua* punishment was anathema certainly did not change in 1815 despite the indisputable emergence of new forms of hierarchy in the international system. New modes of asserting inferiority and superiority assuredly developed at that time, but even in the imperialism of the nineteenth century, the punitive *casus belli* was not invoked. In fact, the new manifestations of hierarchy worked *against* the Grotian logic of punishment, which, as we have seen, was predicated upon the lack of formal hierarchy.

When a state was found to have acted wrongly under the new rules (to have violated a positive, voluntarily undertaken obligation to another state), there was no longer punishment; there were now "countermeasures," but these were available *exclusively* to the injured state. The locus of the response had also changed now. These changes relate to the developments I have been discussing, especially the evolution of sovereignty; from Grotius, the locus of responsibility—and hence punishment—was the nation, the *gens,* the society as a whole, an inclusive concept that entailed that every individual was subject to punishment; in other words, punishment denoted, conquest and subjugation. Now, however, the idea of the state as a rights-bearing and duty-bearing *sui generis* entity separate and distinct from the people and the rulers was coming more securely into place. As we have seen, to the extent that this idea was present in Grotius's work, it was extremely diffuse; we really owe Hobbes and Pufendorf for this concept. Hobbes's "artificial man" (the subject of extensive discussion in Chapter 6) was possessed of rights, and Pufendorf's emendation of Hobbes's account added consideration of the duties a state has distinct from those of the populace or the ruler, but Vattel really solidified things for international law.[57]

With this development, no natural person or persons were responsible for an internationally wrongful act; it was the *state* that was responsible. It was an abstract, juridical (and *stricto sensu* fictitious) entity that was responsible, and even this was the exception during this period. In this period, there was generally no issue of wrongdoing, responsibility, or punishment because of the way in which sovereignty and Positivist Voluntarism were framed, allowing states to largely decide for themselves whether and to what extent to honor their obligations.[58] Concern had moved to the acts and harms a state might inflict upon another state; one state might respond to a harm inflicted upon it by another, but the idea of a general right of any state to "correct" the behavior of another state in a matter that did not materially concern it was becoming progressively more difficult to justify. This is not to say that state behavior changed entirely, but states had to go through more contortions to justify punitive action taken against another state, sometimes by legislating the *other* outside the bounds of international society, and increasingly by reference to what would become humanitarian intervention.

Par in Parem non Habet Imperium

In the account just offered, sovereignty and changes to the dominant conceptualization of sovereignty carry most of the explanatory weight. As stated at the beginning of this chapter, there is no need for another detailed history of sovereignty, but some conceptual clarification and conceptual history of particular components of sovereignty is in order. The dominant doctrinal understanding of sovereignty during the post-Vattelian period is well summed up by Frederick Pollock:

1. States cannot be bound by any rule of international law to which they have not given either their specific or tacit consent.
2. States have the right to be the judge in their own case; that they are subject to no court or tribunal for the interpretation of the rights conferred upon them by international law.
3. States have the right to take the law into their own hands to secure the execution of what they believe to be just.[59]

Along similar lines, Lassa Oppenheim elaborated: "According to the rule *par in parem non habet imperium* no State can claim jurisdiction over another full-sovereign State."[60] "No state is legally superior to another . . . States recognize only one legal superior and that is international law itself."[61]

Pollock's first rule we are already familiar with—it is Voluntarism—"No State can be legally bound without or against its will."[62] Voluntarism progressively restricted state obligations to rules created by states for themselves rather than rules exogenously imposed.[63] By rejecting exogenously imposed rules—even if Grotius, unlike Pufendorf or Leibniz, would not have accepted this characterization of Natural

Law—Voluntarism, as part of the modern understanding of sovereignty, essentially stripped away most of the bases for international punishment. If states had not agreed to particular rules, they could not be bound by them; if they were not bound by them, they could perforce not violate them; if they had not violated them, they could not be punished for their violation.[64] Not bound by the rules prohibiting the acts in question, states committed no wrong by their commission, thereby creating no cause for action. Because states determined for themselves whether they were bound by any given rule, the sort of categorical pronouncements Grotius had made about certain acts being unconditionally subject to punishment could no longer hold, thereby removing a lengthy catalog of purely internal acts from legitimate *casus belli*.

Positivism pushed Natural Law further to the side, by delegitimizing (and indeed denying the reality of) any form or source of law that did not have at its root a definable human act. It also served to abolish any hierarchy of norms (until the recognition of *jus cogens* norms) by putting all forms of law—at least in the international realm—on a par. Thus, states were bound only by Positive Laws to which they had either specifically consented or acquiesced.

Pollock's second rule represents a much greater impediment to international punishment; if we take seriously the idea that states are entitled to be their own judges, the idea of international punishment becomes utterly implausible. Under this rule, if a state does not consent to be bound by another party, correlatively, it cannot be judged by any other party. Classical international punishment was built upon the idea that any nation, as a logical precondition of being able to punish any other in the absence of a tribunal, was entitled to judge the acts of any other. Under the new rule complex, if a state did not consent to be judged, its acts could not be judged, and there could not be legal consequences. Vattel's articulation represents the attitude well:

> It is for each Nation to decide what its conscience demands of it, what it can or can not do; what it thinks well or does not think well to do; and therefore it is for each Nation to consider and determine what duties

it can fulfill towards others without failing in its duties to itself. Hence in all cases it belongs to a nation to judge of the extent of its duty, no other Nation may force it to act one way or another. Any attempt to do so would be an encroachment upon the liberty of Nations . . . If it abuses its liberty it acts wrongly, but other Nations cannot complain, since they have no right to dictate it . . . When differences arise each Nation in fact claims to have justice on its side, and neither of the interested parties nor other Nation may decide the question.[65]

Hegel, in his typical fashion, characterized the matter rather more bluntly:

There is nor Praetor to judge between states; at best there may be an arbitrator or mediator, and even he exercises his functions contingently only, i.e. in dependence on the particular wills of the disputants . . . It follows that if states disagree and their particular wills cannot be harmonized, the matter can only be settled by war.[66]

On its face, Pollock's third rule appears to moot the consequences of the second. It leaves it up to states to "take the law into their own hands." This sounds not at all different from the system Grotius advocated, and appears to make the second rule wholly irrelevant. Closer scrutiny does not bear this out. It is plain that Grotius did not hold nations to be equal.[67] States taking the law into their own hands was not practiced during this period along the lines of classical international punishment, but was (with the exception of humanitarian interventions) undertaken by states to vindicate their own rights (or the rights of their nationals, which were not distinguished from those of the state at that time). Rather than identifying punishment as part of the rules of sovereignty, Pollock links it to reprisal, the topic of the next section. Taking the law into one's own hands certainly implies an act of judgment, but careful discrimination is called for. The judgment is not of the culpability of the other's act. It is not a judgment in a strictly legal sense; rather it is the evaluation of whether you have been harmed (instead perhaps of "injured," which carries specific legal connotations). This may well ultimately be an unsupportable distinction, but it was the operative distinction.

Although P.J. Baker takes great pains to distinguish Oppenheim's position from that of Pollock, the principle *par in parem non habet imperium* relates obviously to Pollock's second rule. No state could be judged by another without its consent, because states as legal equals could not have authority or jurisdiction over each other that had not been granted. If another has legal authority over you, the reasoning went, you are not sovereign.[68] In this system, sovereignty is autonomy, which is equality; as John Westlake put matters, "The equality of sovereign states is merely their independence under a different name."[69]

This rule is not a new development of the era of absolute sovereignty. Yoram Dinstein traces the *par in parem* formulation back as far as the medieval period in a series of Papal Bulls and Glossators' Decretals; deeper roots are easily found.[70] Ernst Kantorowicz points the way back to Justinian, where slightly differently worded formulations are to be found in both the Digest (D.36.1.13.4) and the Codex (C.1.14.4).[71] By missing the earlier formulations, Dinstein is led into error. His reading of the religious materials points to only a temporal dimension of the principle: Prelates were not bound by the rules of their predecessors, and their successors would in turn not be bound by their rules. As peers, one Pope could not bind another later Pope. Dinstein asserts that taking this rule out of its intertemporal context was a later novelty, but it is quite clear from D.36.1.13.4 that the Romans viewed the matter as related to contemporaries: "We must hold that a praetor has no power of command over a praetor, nor a consul over a consul" (*praetorem quidem in praetorem vel consulem in consulem nullum imperium habere*). It is clear from Roman legal practice that this rule had an intertemporal dimension as well; if you look at any sequence of praetorian edicts, imperial *constitutiones*, or comitial *leges* on the same topic, it is immanently clear that the rule was then as it is now that later laws superseded earlier ones.

Dinstein attributes the move away from a temporal understanding of the rule to Dante in *De Monarchia*. *Par in parem* did play a pivotal role in Dante's argument in favor of a universal monarch, but the horizontal understanding was not new with him. However, whether introduction or reintroduction, the effect was to shift usage away from the relations of equals across time to the relation of equals in the same time: "With the conversion of the context of the principle from a vertical line ... into a horizontal plane, its entire role underwent a transformation, and it became possible to adduce it as a bar against one ruler sitting in judgment over his peer."[72] Again, however, Dinstein misses important predecessors. Although not articulated in terms of this specific Latin phraseology, as a matter again of *practice,* the equality presupposed by the formulation has roots before Dante or the Popes in question. Goebel, while noting doctrinal prefigurations in Stoic and early Christian thought, finds a clear history of practice as far back as the early medieval period.

The first element in translating this principle to states was recognized by Goebel as resting in the traditional practice of identifying the state and its ruler: "In international practice and in the law of the period the characteristics of the modern state such as its ... independence, and equality were regarded as the qualities of the king or emperor rather than the political body over which he ruled."[73] By itself, this need not have led to the modern conceptualization; it was further dependent upon the rules of feudalism.

> At the pinnacle of the feudal systems in each state ... was the ruler of the state. From the internal legal point of view the monarch enjoyed an equality with the princes and free lords in respect to ... legal capacity. And the universality of the rules of the feudal system brought it about that in respect to their relations with each other, rulers of separate independent states were guided by principles of equality.[74]

Goebel finds further support for an idea of equality in the prevalent linguistic practices in treaty making with their near uniform invocation of *legales fratres,* which, as he notes, carries a "very striking" implication of equality. "Not only does the word *frater* carry with it an admission of social equality produced by equality of birth, but the use of the word *legalis* before it emphasizes this connotation. *Legalis* is used in the sense of ... the same grade of legal capacity as any other contractant."[75] Goebel is asserting that feudal lords of all ranks were regarded for legal purposes as "peers"; there were obvious power differentials, and there was still a feudal hierarchy of fealty-relations, but he demonstrates that in terms of legal capacities, they were indeed equals and regarded as such. As the transition was made from regarding these juridically equal rulers as sovereign to regarding the states they had once personified as sovereign, that equality was likewise transferred. As Dinstein summarizes the significance of the principle *par in parem non imperium habet*:

> Its literal meaning seems to be relatively simple. The term *imperium* admittedly gives one pause, but its ordinary signification clearly appears to connote power in the sense of authority, control or even dominion. The plain rendering of the principle would, therefore, be: an equal has no power over an equal . . . all States are equally—and mutually— independent, and . . . they must not arrogate to themselves authority over one another.[76]

As we can see in this series of constituent rules of sovereignty, one by one, all of the pillars upon which international punishment was articulated as a just cause for the use of force were eliminated. There were no universal obligations; there were only specific obligations. There were no indefeasible obligations; there were only obligations that could be changed or nullified by state parties.

Natural Law-bound nations were no longer the relevant focus; rights-bearing states defined the era. Although there was no longer any meaningful suggestion that the source of law was anything other than state consent, IR was still rule governed in the post-Vattelian period. In fact, since Pufendorf, it had been insisted that Natural Laws of any sort gave rise only to imperfect obligations—this was a key move in weakening the hold of Natural Law reasoning. As such, they did not allow for coercion in cases of nonperformance. It was only Positive Law that gave rise to perfect obligations, and it was thus only Positive Law that could be enforced. That done, the only grounds left for the just use of force were self-defense and reprisal.

Punishment by Any Other Name?

> An injury done to the Rights, *stricti juris,* of a State, may be vindicated by the employment of a kind of force, which nevertheless falls short of war, and the use of which has always been held to be compatible with the maintenance of general good relations.[77]

It of course remains true that reprisals are acts of war in fact, though not in intention.[78]

To this point in the chapter, we have focused on the broad right of international punishment as articulated by Grotius and the debates it engendered; however, at the outset of the chapter, we mentioned that self-help operated alongside international punishment. One manifestation of self-help, reprisal, while conceptually distinct from punishment, is often spoken of in punitive terms. "Reprisals are punitive in character: they seek to impose reparation for the harm done, or to compel a satisfactory settlement of the dispute created by the initial illegal act, or to compel the delinquent state to abide by the law in the future."[79] While historically part of the *jus ad bellum,* and sometimes taking the same form as punishment, reprisal does not comport with the classical just war tradition's idea of international punishment, and is not necessarily punitive in the sense used previously.

The distinction between punishment and reprisal is subtle. Confusion over the two practices presumably comes from their shared functions. The relevant difference is standing. Punishment, both generically and in the instant context, entails certain rules applicable to all relevant agents. The semantics of punishment implies rules and the violation of rules. Agents are bound by these rules; presumably, rules that all parties know exist. In the case of states (but perhaps not nations historically), these are rules to which all concerned parties are understood to have consented. If an agent violates one of these rules, he, she, or it (in the case of juridical persons) is liable to sanction. In some instances, this sanction is violent. All of this holds for reprisal. Punishment is administered on behalf of the community to which the agents belong. The party inflicting the punishment (even Seneca's "private avenger") is acting as an agent (even if self-appointed) of the community, and not as a party to the dispute. By comparison, reprisal is the use of force *by injured agents* against the party who injured them. Specifically, a reprisal is an *otherwise unlawful* use of force that is tolerated because of the prior injury.[80]

> The injured party [is authorized] to seek full redress and to use force to obtain it if necessary...the injured party has the right to provide for its security in the future and to punish the offender in such a way as to prevent a recurrence of such attacks, and give warning to any others who may be tempted to make similar attacks.[81]

While both punishment and reprisal involve the use of force against parties who have broken rules, the difference lies in the underlying understanding of agency and standing. International reprisal is not a general right to correct *any* other agent's behavior like international punishment, but a right to act against a party that *specifically* harmed you. Therefore, unlike punishment (Grotius's assertions notwithstanding), reprisal does not presume a relationship of authority. Reprisals are specifically within the domain of the interactions of agents of formally equal status.

Reprisal is also a retrospective practice like punishment, but again, there must be a direct link of affected interests between the two parties. Reprisal is not solely retrospective, however; reprisal might be taken coercively to induce the malfeasant into ceasing its injurious behavior while it is still under way, and like punishment, reprisal can serve a deterrent function. Whether reprisal need bring about any outcome other than the infliction of harm is a matter of some confusion. Punishment is usually characterized as performing either a deterrent, rehabilitative, or retributive function.[82] Reprisals can certainly serve a deterrent function. Deterrence is indeed probably implicit in the very idea of reprisal: "If you do that again, we will do this again."[83] This is distinct, however, from the community per se sending the message (even if through an individual agent). Likewise, reprisals are retributive by their very nature. One looks in vain, however, for assertions of a rehabilitative function in reprisal.

The history of reprisal as a practice is far better documented than that of international punishment; conversely, punishment has been better theorized historically.[84] Theodore Woolsey, in his treatment of ancient Greek and medieval European reprisal practices, articulates what has come to be one of the defining categorizations of reprisals:

> The Greeks here present to us two forms of reprisals, the one where the state gives authority to all, or in a public way attempts to obtain justice by force, which is called *general,* and the other, where power is given to the injured party to right himself by his own means, or *special* reprisals . . . [special reprisal] was a recognized method of redress in the middle ages; nor was it strange that a private person, by the leave of his superior, should wage a war of his own, when private wars were a part of the order of things.[85]

What is immediately striking about this formulation is that the focus is on the injuries suffered by *private individuals* and state grants to vindicate them; it is not a matter of interstate violence (perhaps to avoid anachronism, "inter-polity" would be more suitable when discussing Classical Greece).[86] This was indeed the norm for most of history prior to the eighteenth century.[87] Tellingly, in Grover Clark's immensely detailed history of English legal practice with regard to reprisals, purely domestic reprisals are treated alongside those of an international character.[88] Michael Kelly sees the practice arising from "notions of equity—if one was wronged by another's illegal action, then the wronged individual was vested with a right of redress (forcible if necessary) against the wrongdoer."[89]

The sometimes international character of the injuries meant that rulers sometimes granted their citizens the right of reprisal against foreign nationals.[90] In simple cases, reprisal could be carried out in the victim's home state. If the party who injured you happened to be in your state, you could seize their assets or indeed seize their person until you were compensated.[91] More common, however, was the grant to a private citizen to seize the person or possessions of foreign nationals on the seas. As it was often impossible to act directly against the parties who had committed the injury, the right to take reprisals was granted (with certain limitations) against all those of the perpetrators' nationality. In rather Grotian terms, the liability for the initial delict was collective: "The group as a whole— the King and his subjects—was responsible for the acts of its individual members and hence liable for claims resulting from individual acts."[92]

The well-known pairing of *marque* with reprisal grows out of the practice of private reprisal. Clark traces the etymology of the former term to a series of Latinate terms "associated with borders or frontiers," and traces a cognate of *marque* to terms related to "pillage" and "plunder." A "letter of marque," in its earliest usage, was a document granting authorization "solely for seizures to secure compensation for loss." Reprisal is linked etymologically by Clark to "prize," in the sense that the term was used by Grotius in *De Jure Praedae,* and as Clark notes, in admiralty courts. "Others having unlawfully *made prize* of an Englishman's goods, he might, subject to certain conditions, make *re-priz-al*." Over time, the conjoined term gained the connotations it carries in the U.S. Constitution, in which it signifies the grant to a private party to seize "enemy property primarily for the purpose of inflicting injury . . . 'commissions to private men of war.' "[93]

The linking of *marque* and reprisal adventitiously joined two distinct threads of nonstate actor involvement in the *jus ad bellum.* International punishment, which for Grotius extended to nonstate actors such as the Dutch East India Company, was predicated upon a right that inhered in individuals, and therefore did not require governmental grant. *Marque* and reprisal, if they had an advocate like Grotius, might have been asserted to be rooted in an inherent right, but as a matter of practice, they required explicit grants of authority from the state, and were strictly limited in their scope by those same grants.[94]

Like Grotius's theoretical account of punishment, states took over the practice of reprisal from individuals. In this case, the state took the power to engage in reprisals not because it was delegated by individuals upon entering society, but because the practice of private reprisal was causing complications for states: "As private reprisals led to more public warfare involving the state, governments increasingly took control of this doctrine, and it eventually became a recognized right that could only be exercised by the state."[95]

While we alluded earlier to confusions over punishment and reprisal stemming in part from the inconsistent but related uses of "reprisal" in "forcible" reprisals and "belligerent" reprisals, this distinction only speaks to acts of reprisal carried out between states. The categorization we saw in

Woolsey—extrapolated from ancient Greek practice—complicates matters further. Unlike the previous schema, it addresses private reprisals; notably, however, both of Woolsey's categories of reprisal, as well as forcible reprisal, are peace-time measures; "private *reprisals, properly speaking, were not acts of war but were a recognized method of securing justice in time of peace*."[96] Even forcible, that is, interstate reprisal, which may take the form of military assaults and which is certainly hostile, does not constitute a condition of war. Reprisals "constitute a state of war, and are yet considered to be without the pale of the law applicable to war."[97] Henry Wheaton offers something of a hybrid categorization scheme; using the same dichotomy of general and special that Woolsey would later use, Wheaton classified general reprisals as "when a state which has received . . . an injury from another nation, delivers commissions to its officers and subjects to take the persons and property belonging to the other nation, wherever the same may be found."[98] Special reprisals share the same characteristics as Woolsey's account. The transition from the Greek usage to that identified by Wheaton was simple enough: originally a general reprisal authorized any and all citizens to take reprisals; eventually that corporate right was strictly retained and solely exercised by the state. "General reprisals now developed into a political instrument, into a weapon for forcing an adversary to change his policy, into a sanction against another State."[99]

Privateering, which grew out of the ideas of *marque* and reprisal, was—unlike reprisal (except belligerent reprisal)—a wartime activity.[100] There was again, only an adventitious link; previous grants to use force to take prize from the citizens of another state as a response to an injury to you expanded to general grants to all citizens to take prize from any citizens of that other state, but still in response to an antecedent injury.[101] From there, it was a short trip to removing the injury requirement, and employing what had been previously a matter of private law as a tool of statecraft by employing merchantmen not quite as combatants, but giving them general license to take prize from vessels of the enemy state.

In his treatment of reprisal, Clark implicitly relegates inter-state reprisals to the ignoble category of retaliation. "*Retaliation* involves the use of force *to inflict an injury* in return for an injury inflicted; *reprisal* involves the use of force to *secure compensation for a loss by the taking of property*."[102] In none of the various international reprisals surveyed in the literature is force used to secure compensation by the taking of property.[103] There are demands for redress for the initial violation of international law, but those failing, the reprisals are taken so as to hurt the other party and dissuade them from repeating the violation. If we do not want to disqualify state practice from counting as reprisal, we are led to another categorization of reprisals: compensatory reprisals or requitative reprisals.

The definitive modern statement about the role of reprisals in international law and the rules governing resort to reprisal is found in the arbitral decision of the 1928 *Naulilaa* case. In it, the three Swiss arbitrators delineated three requirements for an act of (in this case violent) revenge to constitute a legitimate act of reprisal:

1. A prior unlawful act
2. An unsatisfied request for redress
3. The proportionality of the response[104]

Despite the customary status the arbitrators accorded these criteria some commentators question whether the second criterion has been the norm historically.[105] Clark's extensive historical survey would appear to indicate that it was generally the norm in the case of private reprisals, but to their discredit, the *Naulilaa* arbitrators left their assertion of the customary law status of the requirement undocumented and did not show that states had adopted the requirement they had applied to their nationals to themselves. Robert Tucker insists that the arbitral decision should not be read as requiring attempting to "obtain redress by peaceful means if it is clear that in the circumstances such attempt will prove unavailing."[106]

While the first and second criteria are quite clear-cut empirically—there either was or was not a prior unlawful act, there either was or was not an unsatisfied request for redress—proportionality has proved a more vexed requirement. In the case of private reprisals, the injury could be monetized, and the grantee was given authority to seize that value from the conationals of the malefactor. In the case of international reprisals, injury is not necessarily immediately quantifiable, and the proportionality of the response depends on the purpose of the reprisal. Seeking retaliation—as the Portuguese had in *Naulilaa*—entails one level of appropriate force; seeking to deter the other state from repeating the violation may require a greater amount of violence.[107] "Securing redress suggests that proportionality must be measured by the extent of the damage stemming from the delict, whereas preventing recurrence (deterrence) suggests a more indeterminate standard based on a calculation of what might be necessary to 'teach a lesson.'"[108] There is no way to rigorously gauge the amount of force necessary to "teach a lesson."

Currently, many hold that because of the deliberately narrow framing of Article 2(4) of the UN Charter, violent reprisal is no longer countenanced by international law.[109] "The provisions of the Charter relating to the peaceful settlement of disputes and non-resort to the use of force are universally regarded as prohibiting reprisals which involve the use of force."[110] Principle 1.6 of the *Declaration on Principles of International Law Concerning Friendly Relations and Cooperation among States in Accordance with the Charter of the UN* (inasmuch as it has legal force) reinforces this sentiment: "States have a duty to refrain from acts of reprisal involving the use of force." A reading of the ICJ's dictum in its advisory opinion on *The Legality of the Threat or Use of Nuclear Weapons* (inasmuch as *it* has legal force) further bolsters this view: "Armed reprisal in time of peace . . . are considered unlawful."[111] Nonetheless, the U.S. strikes on Libya (1986) and Iraq (1993) can be read as reprisals, even if they were not presented as reprisals, but rather as legitimate acts of self-defense under Article 51(as might the 1998 strikes on Afghanistan and Sudan). In each case, we have a tit-for-tat exchange of violence for violence. There were demands for redress, and in both cases, the attacks were *more or less* proportionate to the predicate wrong.[112]

To briefly recap the differences: international punishment in the classical tradition was the right of any nation to use violence against any other for the violation of a fundamental rule of law—in that context, the Law of Nature. The punishing nation did not need to have been injured by the violation, nor did it need to have any specific link to the crime or the malfeasant nation. The punishing nation was alleged to have been acting on behalf of the public good, on behalf of international society, in what amounted to an *actio popularis.* International reprisals, by contrast, are not conceptualized as community responses to wrongdoing, but rather one state (note the shift) inflicting proportionate injury upon another state that had previously injured it, or private persons from one state seizing the possessions or persons of the conationals of the party who injured them.

International punishment and reprisal were very similar practices empirically. What enabled the latter to survive the change in normative context was its fit with Positivism. Reprisal did not merely survive, however; by one account, it was pivotal in establishing international law's *bona fides* as law. With only a few outlying exceptions, throughout the post-Vattelian of the *absolute sovereignty-Voluntarism-Positivism complex,* the bindingness of (positive) international law was not in question.[113] That states were bound only by their own consent was, of course, central to this understanding. That states were juridically equal, and thus not subject to one another's authority was also agreed. States could not judge each other, but the need for compliance and means to better ensure compliance remained.

> States acknowledge no common arbitrator or judge, except such as are constituted by special compact...Every state has therefore a right to resort to force as the only means of redress for injuries inflicted upon it by others...Each state is also entitled to judge for itself what are the measures which will justify such a means of redress...[including] by exercising the right of vindictive retaliation (*retorsio facti*) [and] by making reprisals upon the persons and

things belonging to the offending nation until satisfactory reparation is made.[114]

Here again Positivism came into play. In particular that facet of Positivism inaugurated by Hobbes and given canonical expression by Jeremy Bentham and John Austin: the "Command Theory." In it, law is the command of the sovereign backed up by the threat of sanction (punishment).[115] Austin used this definition to deny that international law was law at all.[116]

Hans Kelsen built upon this line of thought, and while ignoring the element of sovereign command, addressed the question of sanction by making reprisal key. Kelsen rescued international law from Austin by showing that reprisals provided a working system of sanction in the absence of a formal hierarchy.[117] Reprisal itself gave international law its *bona fides* as law:

> It is a principle of general international law that a state which considers some of its interests violated by another state, is authorized to resort to reprisals against the state responsible for the violation...Since reprisals are admissible only as reactions against the violation of certain interests of one state by another, they have the character of sanctions; and the violation of interests conditioning the reprisals have the character of a violation of international law, that is, the character of an international delict.[118]

States were still bound by rules, but having defined themselves (and each other through practices of recognition) as sovereign, they no longer claimed a global right to punish one another if rules were broken. Instead, they maintained the right to act directly upon violations of bilateral obligation; they were left, however, without recourse in cases of violations of multilateral obligations that did not specifically injure the interests of any particular state.

Over time, however, reprisals were progressively domesticated, and emphasis was placed on retorsion and legal countermeasures. Eventually reprisal, at least in its forcible forms, now linked with Positivism, followed punishment and has been—in good Positivist fashion—(arguably) legislated out of existence.

With the trajectory of international punishment's rise and fall mapped out, the following chapters each focus on the return of a single constituent element of the old practice. In the next chapter we will analyze the emergence or reemergence of norms the obligation of which is every bit as absolute as those generated by Natural Law, but that have emerged in a specifically Positivist context.

CHAPTER 3

Jus Cogens

The essence of the *jus cogens* doctrine is the recognition of the need to establish common values and standards which will have precedence over state sovereignty and which will accordingly restructure international society.[1]

Peremptory norms are the centerpiece of this book's account of the constitution of international society; while we did acknowledge in the Introduction that there is a certain amount of circularity in using the concept of *jus cogens* to explain the very workings of *jus cogens,* it is important to recognize that in the post-Vattelian period of Positivism's dominance, the very idea of a "hierarchy of norms" in international law, the idea that some norms are "more binding" or "more imperative" than others, or to use Prosper Weil's phrase, the idea of "relative normativity," was treated as if it were conceptually incoherent.[2] The ideas that some norms could not be contracted out of, that some norms could never be legitimately violated, were similarly treated as incoherent. The only limits on states' unfettered freedom of action were understood to be those voluntarily undertaken by states, and those undertakings were understood to always be subject to subsequent renunciation.

By contrast, in the preceding period of classical international punishment, the idea that certain rules were absolutely, exceptionlessly binding and nonderogable was a commonplace. As was intimated in previous chapters, this sort of categorical obligation was a fundament of punitive practice. International punishment was an outgrowth of a particular understanding of Natural Law, and it would not have taken the shape it did were it not for Natural Law's predicate absolutism. The existence of rules that were understood to be superior to the interest of nations (remember, there were no sovereign states proper in this period) and superior to agreements between nations or their rulers or to customary practices of nations was a necessary precondition for the tradition Grotius started. When this idea lost support, punishment necessarily fell by the wayside.

For these reasons, the very introduction of *jus cogens* into the discourse of international law represented a change to the body of international society's fundamental rules. Having discussed *jus cogens* telegraphically in the Introduction, I want to now spend some time examining in more detail how the introduction of this concept into the discourse of international law played a role in the reshaping of the fundamental rules of international society. Unlike the topics of the next two chapters, however, there are few empirical resources to display the workings of this descendant of international punishment. In the absence of significant case law or state practice, the discussion of *jus cogens* in this chapter must primarily operate in theoretical and doctrinal terms—conceptual history and conceptual analysis.[3] While it will prove quite simple to demonstrate the effects of the reintroduction of categorical obligation to international legal *doctrine,* the closest approximations of *practice* are scattered statements made by diplomatic representatives or pleadings and separate opinions in international tribunals.

Deadly Rules

Before turning to the problem of *jus cogens* in international law, however, some terminological clarification is in order because the very semantics of *jus cogens* betray a bit of confusion.[4] In essence, there is a mismatch between the meaning of the term and its meaning-in-use, and while we might follow Ludwig Wittgenstein, and obliterate that distinction, that would not help clarify the conceptual confusions that have resulted from the semantic and lexical issues. The literature and, of course, the *Vienna Convention* use the term "peremptory norm" for *jus cogens;* indeed, the Latin appears only parenthetically in a heading title in the *Vienna Convention.*[5] As will be discussed in the context of *U.S. v Iran,* the word "imperative" is also widely used—it is used rather than "peremptory" in the French text of the *Vienna Convention.* We need to look briefly at the semantic distinctions between these terms and one that I have used repeatedly, "categorical."

"Peremptory," in its legal usage, can be traced back at least as far as Gaius's *Institutes* (second century); in the discussion of exceptions to actions, a distinction is drawn between "peremptory" and "dilatory" exceptions, the former "cannot be evaded."[6] Outside of its legal context, the literal meaning of *peremptorius* was "deadly" or "destructive"; from this base, it was adapted for the law to connote "decisive" or "putting an end to" (a fine euphemism for killing). One cannot help but be somewhat troubled, however, by the idea of deadly or destructive norms. In modern usage, "decisive" and "admitting no refusal" are the dominant aspects of the term's meaning. If a rule is peremptory, compliance with it cannot be refused; if there is a rule in conflict with a peremptory norm, it, rather than the conflicting rule, is decisive.

If death is at the root of "peremptory," violence is at the root of *cogens. Cogo* (of which *cogens* is the present participle) literally meant to "force," to "drive together," "compel," or "constrain." The English "cogent," which derives from *cogo,* still connotes power or force, even if in ordinary language only in the sense of the power or force of a proposition or argument. "Constraining" and "compelling" are still part of things, but none of the aspects of the pragmatics of *cogens* really convey much of what distinguishes *jus cogens* from *jus dispositivum;* all rules are constraining or compelling. The latter term indicates laws that are "subject to the dispensation of parties"; in this case, laws that fall squarely within the traditional Voluntarist understanding of obligation. Lexically, *disponere* relates to the physical placement of objects, and lacks any of the sense of compulsion associated with *cogo.* Some rules are *more* compelling than others, and *some* rules do not permit exception, but there is nothing in the meaning of the term that immediately links *jus cogens* with its meaning-in-use.

Having moved from death to violence, turning to "imperative," we come to command (not leaving either death or violence far behind, however). Imperative shares a root with "empire." *Impero* is to "command" or "rule over"; its cognate, *imperium*, had a both military and legal-political sense, but

> [imperium] originated and was properly at home in the military sphere where it meant the absolute power of the commander in chief to issue and enforce orders, a power which existed with respect to the soldiers under his command as well as to the population in the area of military operations. *It involved the authority to take any measure of coercion the commander saw fit to take, including corporal and even capital punishment.*[7]

In its legal-political sense, higher magistrates of the republic were granted *imperium* (its military roots still in evidence by the magistrate's accompaniment by *fasces*-wielding *lictors*), but it was of a narrower, more restricted sort than that possessed by military commanders. It was, nonetheless, coupled with *coercitio,* the right of coercion and punishment, making violence a near definitional conjunct of *imperium.*

In its modern usage, "imperative" is still closely tied to command; it is no longer associated with office or role, but now characterizes language. The imperative grammatical mood is linked semantically to directive speech acts ("do *x*"), which are associated with hierarchy as a form of rule.[8] "Imperative," like "cogent," would seem to be redundant as a descriptor of a rule. All rules "demand obedience"; while all rules might not be formulated as commands, most *laws* are: laws either command an action or command that an action not be taken. To say that a law or norm is imperative is to say no more than it has law-like qualities.

"Categorical" is a term more often associated with ethics than law, although one does find the term used in liability and in regulatory law. It is Kant's usage of categorical that comes closest to what *jus cogens* means in international law: "absolute," "unconditional," "binding universally" (this last remains the subject of debate with regard to *jus cogens*).[9] Neither "peremptory" nor "cogent" nor "imperative" carry the same sense of the absolute, the unconditional as "categorical"; it alone among these terms entails being exceptionless.[10]

Combining this with "peremptory's" sense of "decisive" gives the full sense of the use of *jus cogens* in international law.

The value of this discussion of the semantics of the language associated with *jus cogens* will become apparent later, when we explore the doctrinal debates associated with it. Lakes of ink have been spilled over the "essence" of peremptory norms in an effort to try to come to grips with the practical import of a few short sentences in two articles of the *Vienna Convention.* Much of the exegetical furor can be attributed to divergences in the underlying understandings of what the words mean apart from their narrow use as legal terms of art.

The Conceptual History of Jus Cogens

Although the idea of peremptory laws was contained in Roman law, the term *jus cogens* appears only once in Justinian's *Digest,* in a passage from Papinian, *Donari videtur quod nullo jure cogente conceditur.*[11] The concept was subsumed under the heading of the *jus publicum,* and is summed up in the rule *Jus publicum privatorum pactis mutari non potest,* which Gaius claimed could be traced back to the Laws of Solon.[12] Gordon Christenson points out an intriguing discordance between our modern understanding and that of the Romans.

> In liberal thought, certain individualistic rights may "trump" other rights or limit the powers of the State. A major difficulty with the *jus cogens* concept . . . is that the tradition from which it is drawn stands this liberal idea on its head . . . In late Roman law . . . the *jus publicum* operated . . . to prohibit private arrangements that would disturb the class structure of the public order. Defections could not be countenanced. Just or unjust, private law arrangements that threatened the ruling order were not permitted to change the status of persons (such as freedmen, slaves, and women) or legal obligations . . . The political and economic demands of slave-owners . . . became non-derogable through legal norms having public and peremptory character.[13]

As a distinct legal-conceptual category, *jus cogens* gained currency when it was reintroduced by the Pandectists.[14] In modern domestic legal systems, the term has been used for quite some time to denote precepts of the *ordre public,* which, like the Roman law category of *jus publicum,* is a set of rules dictating the limits of allowable terms of contract. Such rules cannot be contracted out of *inter se,* and any agreement in violation of these rules is void; express comparison of *jus cogens* in international law and *ordre public* in domestic law is common.[15]

In the classical international law literature, as part of Natural Law, the "Necessary Law of Nations" *(jus necessarium)* was understood to have "existed outside the will of states."[16] The concept paradoxically found its apotheotic expression in Christian Wolff and Emer Vattel, the very authors who—as we saw in the previous chapter—doomed it. Wolff discusses the "Necessary Law" in §4–6 of the *Prolegomena* of his *Jus Gentium Methodo Scientificum Pertractum:*

> We call that the necessary law of nations which consists in the law of nature applied to nations...Since the necessary law of nations consists in the law of nature applied to nations, furthermore as the law of nature is immutable, the necessary law of nations also is immutable. The immutability of the necessary law of nations arises from the very immutability of natural law, and is finally derived from the essence and nature of man...since the necessary law of nations consists in the law of nature applied to nations, and consequently the obligation which arises from the necessary law of nations comes from the law of nature, furthermore, since this obligation itself, which comes from the law of nature, is necessary and immutable, the obligation also...is necessary and immutable; *consequently neither can any nation free itself nor can one nation free another from it.*[17]

Vattel comments similarly in the Introduction to *Le Droit des Gens:*

> It is *necessary,* because Nations are absolutely bound to observe it...Since, therefore, the necessary Law of Nations consists in applying the natural law to States, and since the natural law is not subject to change...it follows that the necessary Law of Nations is not subject to change. Since this law is not subject to change and obligations which it imposes are necessary and indispensable, Nations cannot alter it by agreement, nor individually or mutually release themselves from it. *It is by the application of this principle that a distinction can be made between lawful and unlawful treaties...and between customs which are innocent and reasonable and thus which are unjust and deserving of condemnation...all treaties and customs contrary to the dictates of the necessary Law of Nations are unlawful.*[18]

For both authors, the Necessary Law was one of the three sources of international law along with the Voluntary Law of Nations *(jus voluntarium)* and the Particular Law of Nations (which was further disaggregated into Treaty *[jus pactitium]* and Custom *[jus consuetudinarium]*). As was discussed in the previous chapter, however, despite the august standing both authors seemed to grant the Necessary Law—seeming to place it atop a hierarchy of sources and making it inviolable and unchangeable—its force was only moral. In their accounts, it was paradoxically absolutely binding, absolutely unchangeable, and absolutely *unenforceable.* Nonetheless, the parallels with contemporary understandings of *jus cogens* are readily apparent; both the *jus necessarium* and rules of *jus cogens* status are absolute and nonderogable. The primary differences lie in the attribution of changelessness to the rules of the Necessary Law and the enforceability of modern rules of *jus cogens.*[19]

Centuries after the displacement of the Natural Law tradition, Alfred Verdross introduced the term to modern international law in his 1937 essay, "Forbidden Treaties in International Law."[20] Verdross, in a starkly framed challenge to the regnant Positivism of the time, rejected the contention by "those authors who base the whole international law on the agreement of the *wills* of the states" that "states are free to conclude treaties on any subject whatsoever."[21] By contrast, Verdross found in the general principles of law shared by all legal systems a public order prohibition against agreements *contra bonos mores,* and concluded that because international law counted among its sources "general principles of law recognized by civilized nations," this rule applied to prohibit immoral treaties.[22]

It is important to note that while much current discussion of *jus cogens* is directed toward rules related to the treatment of the individual, Verdross's sole concern was treaties "which *restrict the liberty of one contracting party in an excessive or unworthy manner or which endanger its most important rights.*"[23] For Verdross, an immoral treaty was one that prevented a state from performing the "moral tasks of states": maintenance of domestic order, national defense, "care for the bodily and spiritual welfare of citizens at home," and protecting citizens while abroad.[24] Any treaty constructed to have such effects would be void on its face, and would not give rise to any obligations—at least no obligations related to the portions of the treaty with unlawful / immoral content; there would therefore be no need for the treaty to be voided.[25]

Interestingly, however, Verdross held that should a tribunal declare an immoral treaty to be void, its finding would have "no constitutive, but simply a declaratory character; [the finding] states that no obligation with such contents has ever come into existence."[26] This oversimplifies matters. By conflating the type of speech act and its effect, Verdross missed the constitutive effect of declaring a treaty void. While his *aprioristic* understanding of the invalidity of immoral treaties is a sensible reaction to the "pseudo-positivistic doctrine which denies the prohibition of immoral treaties," he missed the fact that even *if* declaring a treaty void was not what *made* it void, it nonetheless reinforced the fact of its invalidity. Even *if* the invalidity of the treaty came solely from its immorality—ignoring the human-centeredness of Verdross's own account of morality—a declaration that the treaty was void because *contra bonos mores* would reinforce both the strength of the specific moral norm violated and the rule that immoral agreements are void.

Categorical Obligation in a Voluntarist Setting

"The mystery of *jus cogens* remains a mystery."[27]

Decades after Verdross's essay, the *Vienna Convention on the Law of Treaties* formally recognized the existence of peremptory norms, and formally introduced a concept into *positive* international law that many at the Vienna Conference still conceptualized in naturalist terms.[28] In the words of the Vatican's representative, Dupuy, the *Vienna Convention* "sanctioned the 'positivization' of natural law."[29]

Like Verdross's treatment, the *Vienna Convention's* formulation of *jus cogens* only addressed peremptory norms in relation to treaties. Despite the limited focus of the *Vienna Convention's* treatment—not surprising given the subject matter—it should not be supposed that *jus cogens* apply only to treaties. It is currently widely agreed that the ambit of *jus cogens* extends beyond treaties, and that any *act* in conflict with a norm of *jus cogens* is invalid.[30]

> If all treaties in conflict with a peremptory norm are prohibited and, consequently, all acts based on such treaties are unlawful, it seems evident that the outcome is the comprehensive prohibition of *all acts* contrary to peremptory norms... Otherwise, peremptory norms would be made nearly meaningless: the States concerned need only take care not to conclude a formal treaty referring to the violation.[31]

This conclusion is supported by the ILC's commentary: "A rule of *jus cogens* is an overriding rule depriving *any act or situation* which is in conflict with it of legality."[32] Likewise, the Inter-American Court of Human Rights (IACHR) has held: "*Jus cogens* is not limited to treaty law. The sphere of *jus cogens* has expanded to encompass general international law, including all legal acts."[33] While the IACHR's conclusion is correct, its reasoning is somewhat flawed. The applicability to custom and nontreaty acts is not an instance of "expansion"; rather, the basis for the applicability of *jus cogens* is to be found in the syntax of the concept itself: the invalidity of acts in conflict with a peremptory norm is not an *extension* of a rule created by the *Vienna Convention*. In fact, the converse is the case: the invalidity of treaties in conflict with a peremptory norm is a specific instance of the rule of general international law prohibiting contravention of categorical norms. "Once peremptory norms are seen as the product of general international law... it follows that there is no inherent limitation as to the types or categories of acts and transactions to which such norms apply."[34]

Christenson is willing to extend the effect of *jus cogens* to customary law, but not to actions. He reaches this conclusion because he read *jus cogens* as analogous to Hart's secondary rules; performing the function of determining the validity of other rules, *jus cogens* rules do *share* this character, but as was indicated in the Introduction, *jus cogens* always also perform as primary rules by making behavioral prescriptions.[35]

The ICJ has largely refrained from explicit reliance on *jus cogens* in its decisions, and has generally avoided even the use of the term or its synonyms. The concept was clearly at play in *The Hostages Case* (U.S. v Iran), in which the Court did use the language of "imperative norms" with reference to the status of internationally protected persons.[36] In *Nicaragua v U.S.*, while the Court's decision did not declare U.S. actions against Nicaragua during the latter's civil war a violation of *jus cogens,* separate opinions by President Singh and Judge Sette-Camara both treated the UN Charter's rule of nonuse of force as *jus cogens*. President Singh: "The principle of non-use of force belongs to the realm of *jus cogens,* and is the very cornerstone of the human effort to promote peace in a world torn by strife." Justice Sette-Camara: "As far as non-intervention is concerned, in spite of the uncertainties which still prevail in the matter of identifying norms of *jus cogens,* I submit that the prohibition of intervention would certainly qualify as such."[37]

Jus cogens has been invoked by parties in a number of other cases, most notably *Congo v. Rwanda* and the *Genocide Case*. In both cases the Court acknowledged the *jus cogens* character of the genocide prohibition, but it did not bear upon the decisions in either.[38]

Outside of the ICJ, the *jus cogens* character of the prohibition against torture was strenuously emphasized in the ICTY's decision in *Furundzija*.

> It should be noted that the prohibition of torture laid down in human rights treaties enshrines an absolute right, which can never be derogated from, not even in time of emergency (on this ground the prohibition also applies to situations of armed conflicts). This is linked to the fact, discussed below, that the prohibition on torture is a peremptory norm or *jus cogens*. This prohibition is so extensive that States are even barred by international law from expelling, returning or extraditing a person to another State where there are substantial grounds for believing that the person would be in danger of being subjected to torture.[39]

Although not of the character of a judicial decision, in its resolution of the complaint brought against the U.S. by Roach and Pinkerton, the Inter-American Commission on Human Rights found the prohibition against executing minors to be *jus cogens*. "The Commission finds that in the member States of the OAS there is recognized a norm of jus cogens which prohibits the State execution of children. This norm is accepted by all the States of the inter-American system, including the United States."[40]

Notably, in all of these cases, *jus cogens* is linked to acts; in none of them is the tribunal concerned with *jus cogens'* effect on a treaty.

Whether strictly limited to treaties or not, there are a number of characteristics that define *jus cogens;* so far we have primarily focused on their peremptory character, and alluded briefly in the Introduction to the restrictive guidelines for supplanting them; Lauri Hannikainen offers a total of five characteristics parsed from Article 53:

1. They are norms of general international law.
2. They have to be accepted by the international community of states as a whole.
3. They permit no derogation.
4. They can be modified only by new peremptory norms.
5. Peremptory obligations are owed by all states and other subjects of international law to the international community of states.[41]

We do not need to revisit the third and fourth criteria; the next sections will examine propositions one and two. The fifth characteristic, which Hannikainen acknowledges is, strictly speaking, derived from the purposes of *jus cogens,* is about their relationship to obligations *erga omnes* and the question of whether the violation of a peremptory norm enables an *actio popularis.*[42] We will leave these issues for the next chapter.

The Consensuality of Peremptory Norms

A potentially fundamental challenge to Positivist Voluntarism to come from the introduction of *jus cogens* to international law is the suggestion that these are a species of rule that binds states irrespective of their consent to be bound.[43] *Jus cogens* norms must be "accepted and recognized" by the whole international community. What does this mean in practice? Is the consent of every state, is global unanimity required for a rule to attain categorical status, or is there something about *jus cogens* that makes them binding irrespective of state consent? Can they be imposed upon the unwilling, or are they—like regular rules of Positive Law—dependent upon state consent for their obligation?

It seems that the position of the ILC was that peremptory obligation could indeed be imposed.[44] Giorgio Gaja concurs: "Lack of acceptance or even opposition on the part of one or a few States is no obstacle to a norm becoming peremptory."[45] R. St. J. MacDonald makes the even more emphatic claims that the doctrine is nonconsensual, and that "it is the essence of the concept that a peremptory norm is applicable against states that have not accepted the rule."[46] He goes on to claim that this would result in the creation of "a corpus of rules binding on all states and, unlike rules of customary law, they would be binding on even the persistent objector."[47] Milenko Kreça frames the matter in terms reminiscent of Rousseau's *volonté générale,* invoking the "will of the international community," and reifying it, argues that it does not require the "consent of all states."[48]

While there is much weight of *doctrine* in favor of concluding that peremptory norms are not dependent upon state consent, unsurprisingly, this position was not widely held by state representatives at the Vienna Conference.[49] Articulating a strong consensualist view, Hannikainen maintains that peremptory norms require not only consent, but "double consent": "The norm must be both a norm of general international law and it must be recognized as peremptory by the international community of states as a whole."[50]

The most common solution seems to follow along the lines of that offered by Levan Alexidze:

> International community as a whole can mean only one thing: it should comprise all or almost all States of each of the main world political groups of States . . . One or two members of each group cannot affect the will of others directed at establishing a *jus cogens* rule in coordination with other groups. The dissenting States will be under obligation to obey these rules because the international community as a whole cannot allow any two or more States to derogate from international *jus cogens* by mutual consent.[51]

This opens questions, however, about how many states it would take to block a peremptory norm *manqué,* about the specific identification of the "main world political groups" (a simpler task in the *Vienna Convention's* Cold War setting) and their membership.[52]

Talk of imposition and nonconsensuality creates a superficial resemblance to Natural Law, but that is a mere matter of appearance.[53] Of rather greater significance is the fact that should the position that rules of *jus cogens* status can be imposed become widely accepted, it would represent a truly fundamental challenge to Voluntarism, and indeed as the representative from France noted, to the still-dominant understanding of sovereignty.[54]

As matters currently stand, the only recognized means by which a state can become bound by a rule without giving its consent is the subjection of new states to existing customary law (more about this later); as a matter of logic abstracted from actual practice, the conclusion that rules that bind categorically do not require consent is appealing. As this category has been constructed, however, these rules operate no differently than other rules. The matter has not yet been put to the test; the ICJ has never ruled on whether any rule is *jus cogens,* or whether a *jus cogens* rule (presumably from custom or treaty) is binding on any given party. So, while the idea that categorical rules do not require consent is in one regard compelling, the fact is that as matters currently stand, there is no evidence of willingness on the part of states to subject themselves to rules of any sort to which they have not consented—the current (Voluntarist) standard.

The Universality of Peremptory Norms

One of the central questions surrounding *jus cogens* is whether these categorically binding rules are also universally binding, and if they are, whether they are universally binding necessarily, or only adventitiously. If *jus cogens* rules are expressly part of "general international law," the argument goes, then they are generally applicable to all "or at least great majority of" international legal persons.[55] "Peremptory norms must be general because only the international community as a whole can create norms that are inalterable in the eyes of community members when they are not acting as a whole."[56]

There is some ambiguity regarding whether "general" implies "universal"; as Hannikainen notes, the *Vienna Convention* uses both terms (although she elides the fact that "universal" appears elsewhere in an unrelated discussion), but there is no consensus among scholars.[57] Given the otherwise absolute character of *jus cogens,* however, it would seem at first impression that they must operate *erga omnes.* For Christos Rozakis, while a general rule is not necessarily a universal rule, "in the sense that it is not considered as binding by all . . . the members of the community . . . it tends to become so."[58] Alexidze, apparently as given over to notions of the *volonté générale* as Kreça, argues for the supremacy of the "common coordinated will of the international community of states."[59] He concludes that the reach of peremptory norms of general international law must be universal because "the international community as a whole cannot allow individual States to undermine the legal order established by this community."[60]

As was the case with the question of the consensuality of categorical obligations, the matter comes to the construction of the category; if *jus cogens* were constructed as nonvoluntary, nonconsensual, then they would bind universally, but because they have been constructed in a manner in which the Voluntarist rules of the game still dominate, they cannot be *necessarily* universal simply because of the character of the obligation they impart. As matters currently stand, if a rule is to bind universally, it must do so, not because it has been constructed as binding categorically, but because it has been specifically constructed as binding universally, and has been accepted universally. That universal bindingness will similarly end once the consent to be bound ends.

How Things Get Categorical

All human beings carry about a set of words which they employ to justify their actions, their beliefs, and their lives. These are the words in which we formulate praise of our friends and contempt for our enemies, our long-term projects, our deepest self-doubts and our highest hopes. They are the words in which we tell, sometimes prospectively and sometimes retrospectively, the story of our lives. I shall call these words a person's "final vocabulary"...It is "final" in the sense that if doubt is cast on the worth of these words, their user has no noncircular argumentative recourse. Those words are as far as he can go with language; beyond them is only helpless passivity or a resort to force.[61]

[*Jus cogens* rules] do not exist to satisfy the needs of the individual states but the higher interest of the whole international community. Hence these rules are absolute.[62]

[*Jus cogens* rules] derive from the principles that the legal conscience of mankind deem absolutely essential to coexistence in the international community.[63]

The opening wedge in explaining how dispositive rules can become categorical is provided by the recognition that despite their categorical character, rule of *jus cogens* are, in fact, subject to change, and we can thus infer some recognition of a limited contingency: because norms of *jus cogens,* unlike laws of nature, are changeable, we can infer that they are human constructions, and therefore contingent. Because they are contingent human constructions, their categorical normativity must be explainable by reference to human acts. This means we must explain the basis for the *categorical* obligation of international norms of *jus cogens.* They are binding in the first instance because they are duly promulgated rules; we must determine why, in contrast to "regular" rules of dispositive character, they are absolutely, unconditionally binding.[64]

The underlying problem with the debates over *jus cogens* is that partisans have been framing the search for the source of their absolutely binding character wrongly—when they bother to do so at all. When we ask why some rules create categorical obligations, the answer is very simply that they have this character because we *say* they do; we *make* them that way, and although we must always bear in mind the contingency of this attribution, we need nothing else.

International society's *jus cogens* rules reflect its final vocabulary—the vocabulary that is shared by the international community—to the extent it is appropriate to attribute beliefs to such a notional community.[65] "The international *jus cogens* reflects the authentic needs of the international community."[66]

This is precisely what is at work in Myres McDougal and Michael Reisman's characterization of *jus cogens* in terms of the international community's most intensely sought after demands.[67] My approach is likewise analogous to the terms in which Nicholas Onuf and Richard Birney characterize *jus cogens:* "Such principles stand as generally understood and accepted characterizations of the abiding concerns of the international community . . . [they] are simultaneously the decisive symbols of the international legal order and its constitutive propositions."[68]

When an interlocutor casts doubt on the unjustifiability of slavery or genocide, there is no way to argue with them in terms outside of the vocabulary in which we have framed our categorical injunction; we have no way to argue on behalf of our final vocabulary that does not employ terms taken from the vocabulary itself. It is, Rorty says, as far as the user can go with language; we "have exhausted our argumentative resources"; as Wittgenstein said, our "spade is turned."[69] There is no neutral, universal, meta-vocabulary within which we can step out of our respective vocabularies and debate the matter in neutral, transcendental terms; "nothing can serve as a criticism of a final vocabulary save another such vocabulary."[70]

Jus cogens are, to elaborate, the final vocabulary of the ephemeral international "we" introduced previously. A final vocabulary that is global in scope, based on a "we" that is likewise global in scope, is going to be vanishingly thin; the debates between communitarians and cosmopolitans only serves to highlight this.[71] I do not consider this a problem, because the list of norms that are candidates for *jus cogens* status, and hence universal peremptoriness, is likewise extremely limited.

We do not necessarily want the majority of international legal rules—any more than the majority of domestic rules—to generate categorical obligations, because every change of status of a rule or law from dispositive to peremptory entails a reduction in the agency of all parties concerned (not necessarily an *in se* bad contrary to certain strands of liberal thought), but also, and more importantly, because this change makes the rule or law in question less dynamically responsive to novel situations that do not fit neatly within existing legal frameworks. A society in which every rule was absolutely exceptionless is a terrifying prospect to all but those of the most absolutist mind-set. The great insight of the Legal Realists was to make very clear that static laws (and static understandings of the law) are far too reified to meet the needs of dynamic social situations.[72] Encountering novel situations is part of what changes final vocabularies, part of what makes laws in general change, and presumably what would result in the supplanting of a peremptory norm.

Although I have asserted that *jus cogens* are the bedrock legal norms of our "thin" cosmopolitan morality, I do not want simply to equate *jus cogens* with international morality *simpliciter,* because, whatever else, these norms are *law,* and law—unlike morality—does not countenance a distinction between "ought" and "must."[73] Peremptory norms may reflect morality or sentiments—one would be hard pressed to find any high-level principles of law that do not—but they are also part of the Positive Law.[74] By rooting *jus cogens* in a global final vocabulary, I do not reduce international law to international ethics, but want instead to argue that it is the very categorical character and bindingness *of* these laws that has a moral basis. They are "more binding" than regular rules because in our moral vocabulary, we cannot even conceive of legitimate grounds for their violation whatever the circumstances.

Looming in the background, however, are the consequences of Rorty's injunction that we be ironic about even our final vocabularies, and realize that although they are nominally "final," they can change, and understand that what we regard today as our most deeply held beliefs might be revised tomorrow. When coupled with the rules of Article 64 of the *Vienna Convention,* this opens the door *ex hypothesi* to the possibility that the absolute prohibitions of genocide and slavery might one day be put aside for other, conflicting norms rooted in another, conflicting final vocabulary. This is obviously a consequence that is distasteful in the extreme, one against which Rorty cannot offer any argument, and part of the attraction of Natural Law reasoning. Who we are—people, societies, the society of societies, which believe that there is no possible justification for these proscribed acts—is not rooted in anything necessary, but is rather wholly contingent. It is not *true* in any deep sense that these things we reject unconditionally have been rejected because they are *wrong* in any deep, transcendental sense. We have not *discovered* their wrongness, because their "wrongness" is not like a material fact of the physical world; we have ascribed wrongness to the things we unconditionally reject; we have constructed their wrongness, and like any ascription or any construction, it can change. Because only one final vocabulary can replace another, there may be little cause for concern on this count; we would have to be *talked* out of our current final moral vocabulary, by having our beliefs and practices redescribed. Unfortunately, such a world is imaginable, but what is important to take from Rorty's views on irony and final vocabularies is that when someone attempts to make a "reasonable" argument for genocide, we will not defeat them by argumentation, but only by redescription, by redescribing their practices and beliefs in ways that illustrate their cruelty and baneful consequences.

Although the distinction between argumentation and redescription is imperfect—redescription as Rorty presents it, is after all a rhetorical strategy, and hence designed to *persuade* people to believe differently than they currently do—the point is that there cannot be argumentation *per se* across final vocabularies because they do not share simples or primitives.

> Plato thought that the way to get people to be nicer to each other was to point out what they all had in common—rationality. But it does little good to point out . . . [to the Serbs] that many Muslims and women are good at mathematics or engineering or jurisprudence. Resentful young Nazi toughs were quite aware that many Jews were clever and learned.[75]

If you want to persuade me that it is wrong to eat animals because they have souls, and that it is a *prima facie* wrong to eat anything with a soul, we would reach an impasse if the notion of a soul was not part of my final vocabulary, or if I were conceptually aware of "soul," but rejected the possession of a soul as a morally relevant characteristic. If I wanted to persuade you to abandon the genocidal practices your state has engaged in against its minorities, invoking the innate wrongness of exterminating a people will be pointless if your final vocabulary does not include your victims within the category of "people," or more broadly, if your vocabulary does not countenance the aggregation of discrete humans as a "people," and ascribe an independent dignity, worth, and claim to continued existence to the aggregation.

> For most white people, until very recently, most black people did not so count [as human]. For most Christians, until the seventeenth century or so, most heathens did not so count. For the Nazis, Jews did not count. For most males in countries in which the average annual income is less than two thousand pounds, most females do not so count. Whenever tribal and national rivalries become important, members of rival tribes and nations will not so count . . . Such people are *morally* offended . . . by the suggestion that they treat people whom they do not think of as human as if they were human.[76]

Conclusion

The introduction (or perhaps reintroduction) of the concept of *jus cogens* to international law has challenged pillars of the existing complex of practices and defining rules of international society: we now recognize—at least in principle—a hierarchy of legal rules; Voluntarism is, if not directly under challenge, at least no longer automatically *assumed* with regard to all rules and all rule types within international law. Like international criminal law and its cognate, the universality principle (to be discussed in Chapter 5), there are now rules of international society at large that are recognized as outweighing a state's concern for its sovereignty and its sovereign prerogatives. This has obviously not pushed things back to the Grotian punitive ethos and its related normative complex.

There is nothing *per se* punitive about *jus cogens,* but neither was there anything necessarily punitive about the *jus necessarium.* In both cases the norms fitting within these categories provided the bases for subsequent action: the Necessary Law of nations, provided the basis for the punitive use of force, and ultimately, conquest. In the case of *jus cogens,* it remains to be seen if they provide the basis for the remaining new manifestations of the old practice.

Although this chapter touched on the question of the universality of *jus cogens* rules' obligation, the next chapter is concerned primarily with obligations that are expressly universal and the consequences of their violation, namely, does the violation of an obligation *erga omnes* give universal standing to take legal action?

CHAPTER 4

Obligations *Erga Omnes* and the *Actio Popularis*

Erga omnes rules expand the scope of possible claimants in certain situations, to protect key common interests where traditional rules of standing are insufficient to do so.[1]

If violations of obligations *erga omnes* did not trigger any special rights of response, the concept, at least for the purposes of law enforcement, would be of rhetorical value only.[2]

Chapter 3 addressed categorical obligations, but showed that simple assertions of the universality of *jus cogens* rules did not fit within the current normative complex, which is still predominantly wed to the specificity of obligations. This chapter turns to the reemergence of obligations that are conceptualized not as bilateral, as has been dominant under Positivism, but as obligations that are owed generally; they are obligations *erga omnes*.[3]

> The term "*erga omnes* obligation" is not the generic term of a set of bilaterally structured obligations, but of one integrally structured obligation linking states upon which the obligation is incumbent to the international community as a whole and, thus to all other states. Therefore, the involvement of *erga omnes* issues transgresses the traditional bilateral approach to the settlement of disputes.[4]

The obligation *erga omnes* is owed by a state to the entire international community; *in principle* it confers the right upon any state to hold another *legally* responsible for the obligation's fulfillment; "when speaking of obligations *erga omnes* the essential idea is not that the obligations are owed to all States, but that in case of the breach of such an obligation the corresponding 'rights of protection' are in possession of each and every State."[5] The general argument in favor of the recognition of the power of these obligations works along the following lines: if an obligation *erga omnes* is owed to the community at large and to each member of the community, then unless the community itself has some mechanism by which to ensure its observance, that function must devolve to its members—an argument not unlike Grotius's analysis of enforcement (punishment) in the State of Nature. If we do not allow that *erga omnes* obligations grant any member of the community the right to take legal action in the case of their violation, then such a class of obligation is either meaningless, not actually an obligation, or merely hortatory; in the absence of *actio popularis* in vindication of a breach, we are confronted with the intolerable paradox of universally binding norms that are universally unenforceable. As theoretical points, these assertions are unassailable, but as we will see, this "right of protection" has been limited in practice, and those limitations have come precisely from the same Positivist Voluntarism that caused the fall of classical international punishment.[6]

After an initial analysis of the idea of the obligation *erga omnes;* its cognate, the *actio popularis;* and their relationship to classical international punishment, we turn to the consequences of violating obligations that are owed to all other states. In that section, we look first at bringing a case before the ICJ against a violating state, and then turn to taking direct countermeasures against the offending state. In the final section we analyze the relationship between obligations of this sort and *jus cogens.*

The Link to Classical International Punishment

The Grotian / Lockean understanding of international punishment is predicated upon an apparently simple equation: Natural Law was categorically and universally binding (*jus cogens* and *erga omnes*); because Natural Law was universally binding, but lacked a universal authority to enforce it, anyone might enforce it by punishing violators (undertake an *actio popularis*). In the "original" State of Nature, that responsibility / right fell to individuals; in the (second) State of Nature in which nations found themselves, it fell to nations themselves to enforce Natural Law. To restate the matter slightly, the categorical obligations created by Natural Law were understood to operate *erga omnes;* their violation allowed any party to undertake an *actio popularis* in their vindication. The entire edifice of classical international punishment was reliant upon this equation.

In contrast to classical international punishment, the emphasis in the contemporary understanding of obligations *erga omnes* is not on violations of exogenously imposed Natural Law punishable by any and all, but rather positive, voluntarily undertaken obligations to *all,* legally actionable (in principle) by *any*. In principle, every state has a legal interest in the observance of obligations *erga omnes;* thus, any state may take legal action—either seeking adjudicatory remedies or directly engaging in legal countermeasures—to ensure compliance with an obligation *erga omnes*.[7]

Legal action taken by a state in vindication of a general obligation, taken "on behalf of the international community because it has an interest in the preservation of world order as a member of that community" is an *actio popularis,* the fundamental element of classical international punishment— borrowed from Roman legal practice—that endowed all states with standing to punish violators of the Natural Law.[8] Rooted in Roman law, it has also found expression in multiple modern domestic legal systems.[9] *Digest* 47.23.1 held that the *actio popularis* was a legal procedure "which protects the rights of the party who brings it, as well as those of the people," while *Pandects* 47.23 stated, "Popular actions are those by which a right of the people is defended."[10] There was no single *actio popularis;* rather it was a family of *actiones,* "the distinguishing feature of which was that the plaintiff . . . need not have been personally involved in or affected by the act upon which the action was based."[11] Unlike the later punitive uses to which the concept was put by Grotius and Locke, in Roman law, *actiones populares* were not part of criminal law, but rather part of the Law of Obligations, and were applicable to a wide range of subjects: falsifying praetorian edicts; throwing, hanging, or pouring things from windows in a dangerous manner; the safe navigation of waterways; the violation of tombs; tampering with property lines; and seeking the release of someone unlawfully enslaved.[12] Comparing it to contemporary law's class action, William Aceves has characterized the *actio popularis* as representing "the most attenuated form of group litigation, where the individual applicant seeks relief on behalf of a larger community. In these cases, there is no indication that the applicant is authorized to speak on behalf of this community. Indeed, the applicant may not have even suffered the underlying injury experienced by the larger community."[13]

Although in both Roman law and Grotian / Lockean theory the linkage between universally held obligations and the universal right to take action in case of their violation was clear-cut and unproblematic (or at least treated *as if* it were), modern international law has not treated things in this way. In the simple version of the story, the *actio popularis* was famously mentioned and dismissed by the ICJ in the *South-West Africa* cases as something "unknown to international law"; a few years later, in *Barcelona Traction,* the Court allowed that there might be obligations owed to the international community as a whole that could be acted on by any state when violated; sometime later, when given an opportunity to put this idea to the test in *East Timor,* however, the Court balked. Matters are rather more complicated than this simple narrative would indicate.

Obligations *Erga Omnes* Before the ICJ

Erga omnes rules expand the scope of possible claimants in certain situations, to protect key common interests where traditional rules of standing are insufficient to do so.[14]

Those we might label enthusiasts of the role of the obligation *erga omnes* and the *actio popularis* essentially operate from the classical equation; with regard to countermeasures, the evidence seems to support them. With regard to taking disputes to the ICJ, however, other rules that work directly against this equation must be taken into account. The ICJ is governed by certain predicate rules of standing and interest, which, while not considered normatively superior, are treated by the Court as procedurally prior. In other words, if the requirements of these procedural rules are not met, the case will not be heard because the complaining state will be judged to lack the requisite standing to bring the claim *(South-West Africa)*, or the case will not be heard because the respondent state or a third party whose interests are involved has not made the requisite grant of jurisdiction to the Court *(East Timor)*.[15]

Before engaging in the nuances of these issues, a brief exposition of the primary cases around which this debate has largely been framed is in order. Beginning in 1950, the Court faced a series of apartheid-related cases. In 1950, the Court rendered an advisory opinion at the request of the UN General Assembly on the question of whether the 1920 League Mandate over South-West Africa was still in force, and whether it could be converted into a UN Trusteeship over the objections of the League mandatory, South Africa.

To help ensure that South Africa would comply with its legal obligations, the General Assembly "in Resolution 1361 (XIV) of 17 November 1959, drew the attention of member States to the possibility of their bringing a contentious case against South Africa based on the submission to the jurisdiction contained in the Mandate."[16] Liberia and Ethiopia brought actions against South Africa in 1960 for its failure to adhere to the terms of the League Mandate.[17] Liberia and Ethiopia had invoked the notion of the "sacred trust of humanity" from the League's Charter (as well as the less exotic jurisdictional provisions of the Mandate agreement) to justify their claim to standing, arguing that because of this "sacred trust of humanity" *all* states had an interest in seeing South Africa's obligations fulfilled.[18] If Liberia and Ethiopia had an interest in seeing the obligations fulfilled, they reasoned, they should then *a fortiori* have legal standing to ensure that the obligations were fulfilled.

Although the majority ruled against South Africa's preliminary objections to the Court's jurisdiction, the Court's president, Bohdan Winiarski, in his dissent suggested that the idea of the *actio popularis* underlies Liberia and Ethiopia's claim, and challenged the validity of such a basis. "Reference has been made in this connection to an institution under the old Roman penal law known as *actio popularis* which, however, seems alien to . . . international law."[19] By contrast, in his separate opinion, Judge Jessup asserted, "International law has long recognized that States may have legal interests in matters which do not affect their . . . material interests."[20]

When the Court delivered its decisions in the merits phase of the case, in perhaps its most lamented decision, the ICJ denied Liberia and Ethiopia standing to make claims against South Africa, holding them to lack any legal interest in the matter.[21] The Court, adopting the logic of President Winiarski's dissent in the Preliminary Objections phase, denied that international law provided in any way for "an *actio popularis*, or right resident in any member of the international community in vindication of a public interest."[22] Indeed, the majority (constituted by Winiarski's tie-breaking vote) held that the *actio popularis* was "not known to international law."[23] If Liberia and Ethiopia were not *specifically* injured by South Africa's actions, the majority held, or if South Africa were not in violation of an obligation *specifically* owed to Liberia and Ethiopia, then they could not bring charges against South Africa.[24] Essentially, the matter came to a conflict between the rules of jurisdiction and the rules of standing, and the Court found that the applicants lacked standing to bring their claim because of their lack of clear legal interest in the matter.

A number of objections immediately present themselves to the Court's conclusion. Most obvious is the empirical falsity of the assertion that the *actio popularis* was "unknown to international law." Egon Schwelb ably demonstrates the abundance of treaties, known at the time of both the conclusion of the Mandate agreement and *South-West Africa,* that provided for *actiones populares,* if not by name.[25] Of course, as Christian Tams notes, no party invoked or asserted the *actio popularis;* "they simply interpreted Article 7(2) differently."[26]

Four years later, in the *Case Concerning the Barcelona Traction, Light and Power Company, Limited* (Second Phase) the Court showed itself to be somewhat more receptive to such ideas. Barcelona Traction was a Canadian corporation operating in Spain that at the time of the precipitating incidents was owned by a majority of Belgian shareholders. It claimed to have been the victim of unlawful acts by the Spanish government driving it into bankruptcy and resulting in the seizure of its assets that were then transferred to Spanish interests. Canada initially was involved in the matter but withdrew after a short time. Subsequently, the Belgian government decided to take up the matter asserting it had an interest in protecting the rights of its nationals (both natural persons and juristic persons) as a measure of diplomatic protection.[27]

The Court ultimately denied that Belgium had legal standing to bring the case because the corporation retained its Canadian (legal) nationality despite the nationality of its shareholders. Although the Court denied the underlying claim in *Barcelona Traction,* the Court did acknowledge that there might exist circumstances under which the question of nationality might not apply; there might be certain obligations that if violated, any state might have standing to seek their vindication. In other words, the Court acknowledged the existence of universally held obligations and the—at least theoretical—possibility of universal standing to vindicate them, famously stating:

> An essential distinction should be drawn between the obligations of States towards the international community as a whole, and those arising vis-à-vis another State . . . By their very nature, the former are the concern of all States. In view of the rights involved, *all States can be held to have a legal interest in their protection;* they are obligations *erga omnes.*[28]

Unfortunately for the Belgian shareholders, the violated obligations were not of this nature, but were of the less exotic bilateral sort for which a state must demonstrate its right "to bring a claim in respect of the breach of such an obligation."[29] Christian Hillgruber suggests that in setting matters out in this fashion, the ICJ "seized the first available opportunity to distance itself as quickly as possible" from its decision in *South West Africa.*[30] Tams rightly sounds a note of caution that nothing in this famous passage indicates that the Court felt that "this legal interest could be vindicated by way of ICJ proceedings."[31]

Barcelona Traction is important for acknowledging the category of obligations *erga omnes,* even if such obligations were not operative in the subject matter of the case. *Contra* its previous decision in *South-West Africa,* the Court conceded at least the existence of obligations owed to all and actionable by all. It is a mistake, however, to treat the Court's acknowledgment as entirely novel:

> Contrary to a popular perception, standing to protect general interests was much discussed in the years preceding the emergence of the *erga omnes* concept. The growing recognition, in the course of the twentieth century, of multilateral obligations transcending the bilateral relations between pairs of States put pressure on the allegedly "bilateral-minded" system . . . The problem . . . arises wherever a State violates multilateral obligations that cannot be performed in relation to one other State, and which therefore are not . . . "bilateralisable."[32]

The term itself was used prior to *Barcelona Traction,* as Tams notes, primarily with regard to the effects of treaties on non-party states (third parties)—treaties might have *erga omnes* effects.[33]

Hopes that the ICJ would clearly enunciate a right to vindicate obligations *erga omnes* were set back in the *East Timor* case, albeit again on procedural grounds, but importantly the procedural issue had to do with a state's sovereign right to be subject to the Court's jurisdiction only when it had so consented—a Positivist-Voluntarist strike at the very core of the ideas of the obligation *erga omnes* and the *actio popularis.*[34]

In this case, Portugal made a number of assertions of illegal conduct on the part of Australia arising from its conclusion in 1989 of a treaty with Indonesia dividing the continental shelf off East Timor, but, as Christine Chinkin noted, Portugal "is not a party to the Timor Gap Treaty; it must therefore demonstrate that it has a legal interest in the case it has commenced against Australia."[35] Portugal's position was that "in making and in implementing the 1989 treaty [Timor Gap Treaty] Australia had infringed the rights of the East Timorese to self-determination and to permanent sovereignty over natural resources and Portugal's rights as Administering Power of East Timor."[36] Portugal presented the relevant rights of the East Timorese as opposable *erga omnes* and thus creating obligations *erga omnes* for which Portugal had standing to bring a claim. "It is arguable that where the third-party interests are those of the broader international community they should counterbalance the procedural right of an individual third State not to be subject to the ICJ's jurisdiction without its consent."[37]

Australia made a number of objections to the admissibility of Portugal's claims, the most important of which was that any decision the Court might render would require it to pass judgment on the conduct of Indonesia [in this case, its takeover of East Timor in 1975–1976] over which it had not been granted jurisdiction.[38] In the event, the ICJ did acknowledge the *erga omnes* character of the right to self-determination, and the concomitant obligation to respect it—"Portugal's assertion that the right of peoples to self-determination . . . has an *erga omnes* character, is irreproachable"—but because it could not legally judge the behavior of Indonesia, and without doing so, could not render a decision, it declined to hear the case.[39] In a blow to the possibility of the *actio popularis* even in defense of such a fundamental right, the Court held that "the *erga omnes* character of a norm and the rule of consent to jurisdiction are two different things. Whatever the nature of the obligations involved, the Court could not rule on the lawfulness of the conduct of a State when its judgment would imply an evaluation of the lawfulness of the conduct of another state that is not party to the case. *Where this is so, the Court cannot act, even if the right in question is a right* erga omnes."[40] Procedure and Positivist Voluntarism again trumped universality and status of obligation; "normative status [is] irrelevant in matters of consensual jurisdiction."[41] Tams is less despairing, noting that the Court did not rule on the question of Portugal's standing to bring a claim based on the violation of an *erga omnes* obligation; "the Court held that *even if* the right in question is a right *erga omnes*, it could not decide the case. The use of the proviso, 'even if' seems to suggest that, but for the absence of an indispensable third party, Portugal would have been entitled to respond to the alleged breach of an obligation *erga omnes*."[42]

As was the case in *South-West Africa,* the Court's decision has been subjected to a number of criticisms. We may broadly group them in two categories: legal and ethico-political. The latter category is focused primarily on the Court's unwillingness to give East Timorese self-determination its proper due ("The International Court in a Timorous Mood," "Self-Determination Undermined," "The Illegal Use of Force Validated?"). This line of criticism faults the Court for placing procedural rules above primary rules it has acknowledged as being of higher normativity.[43] This line of criticism reflects what was earlier called the enthusiastic approach to the *erga omnes / actio popularis* equation, which itself reflects (albeit unconsciously) the classical punitive ethos.

The other line of criticism focuses on the legal logic of the Court's decision. The ICJ's "indispensable third party" rule was taken from its earlier decision in the *Monetary Gold* case, in which it had held that the "Court would not rule on questions where the legal interests of a State not before the Court 'would form the very subject matter of the decision.' "[44] The aptness of applying the *Monetary Gold* rule regarding "indispensable third parties" is challenged by critics, and Portugal had preemptively asserted its inapplicability. Vaughan Lowe distills the inapplicability arguments to three. First, the fact that it was only Australia's conduct in disregarding Portugal's asserted "exclusive treaty-making power in relation to East Timor, and not Indonesia's conduct" that was being challenged. Second, Australia's objective responsibility to respect the East Timorese right of self-determination irrespective of any other state's conduct. Third, "the Security Council and General Assembly, acting within their competence, had already decided that States must not recognize Indonesian authority of East Timor, so that the Court had no need to decide that question itself."[45]

Dissatisfaction with decision is perhaps best summed by Christine Chinkin.

> Substantive law developments towards the acceptance of the related concepts of obligations owed *erga omnes* and non-derogable norms

of *jus cogens* have not been matched by procedural flexibility. Indeed the ICJ explicitly distinguished between the *erga omnes* nature of the norm of self-determination and the jurisdictional requirement of consent. Incorporation of such substantive principles, backed by procedures for implementation, would engender a communitarianism within international law that would move its development beyond the traditional bilateral framework . . . The *East Timor* case retreats from any such radical restructuring of the hierarchy of international norms by favoring procedural requirements over substantive change. Ultimately the beneficiary is the alleged wrongdoer, Indonesia, which remains sheltered by its sovereignty.[46]

What we can see from the previous discussion of the treatment of obligations *erga omnes* (and the *actio popularis*) before the ICJ is a trajectory of rather timid progress in which Positivist notions of Voluntarism and bilateralism have retarded more aggressive application of this chapter's focal concepts. Maurizio Ragazzi frames the dominant attitude rather brusquely: "The concept of obligations *erga omnes* does not necessarily imply the existence of a sort of *actio popularis*. In other words, the concepts of obligations *erga omnes* and *actio popularis,* though associated in some respects, are distinct and independent of one another."[47] There must be a specific grant of jurisdiction, a specific authorizing norm for any exercise of the *actio popularis*.[48] The Court has now repeatedly shown its theoretical willingness to hear a claim brought by a noninjured party in vindication of a breached obligation erga omnes, but *only* subject to its own purely Voluntarist rules of standing. In this regard, we can see that the punitive ethos is still reflected in the acceptance—albeit not by name—of the *actio popularis,* but not to such a degree as to outweigh Positivist procedural rules built around the regime of sovereignty. Matters look remarkably different when taken out of The Hague, however.

Obligations *Erga Omnes* and Countermeasures

The other mode of enforcing obligations *erga omnes* that states have adopted hews much closer in some regards to classical international punishment than seeking legal remedies at the ICJ. Like Grotius's and Seneca's "private avenger," states have taken it upon themselves to act directly against others that have violated these obligations. Unlike the "private avenger" of classical international punishment, however, the recourse is not to violence, but to legal countermeasures. Countermeasures are allowable nonperformances of international obligations by a state that has been specifically injured by another's commission of an "internationally wrongful act in order to induce that State to comply with its obligations."

Before analyzing state practice in undertaking countermeasure to vindicate obligations *erga omnes,* a brief *précis* on countermeasures generally is in order. Traditionally, countermeasures, like the obligations they are utilized to protect, have been conceptualized in strictly bilateral terms. They are thus more akin to reprisal as discussed in Chapter 2 than to punishment, although, as Nigel White and Ademola Abass note, "the ILC, together with the International Court of Justice, distinguish countermeasures from reprisals by saying that countermeasures are instrumental while reprisals are punitive."[49] As we saw in Chapter 2, however, that distinction does not hold.

The rules governing resort to countermeasures today are to be found in Articles 49–54 of the *Articles on State Responsibility.* Countermeasures should last only as long as the original violation, and may not involve the threat or use of force, the violation of fundamental human rights, or the violation of *jus cogens,* and must be proportionate to the original violation. The state targeted by the countermeasures must be notified, and there must be an accompanying offer to negotiate. They must cease once the dispute appears before a dispute-settlement body.

With regard to the standing of noninjured parties to undertake countermeasures, the *Articles* allow noninjured states to invoke the responsibility of a violating state if "the obligation breached is owed to the international community as a whole" (Art. 48), and in addition to invoking the violating state's responsibility, Article 54 allows them to "take lawful measures." It thus seems that although traditionally a bilateral self-help measure, international law does now recognize the right of third parties to undertake countermeasures in vindication of obligations *erga omnes.*[50]

Matters seem fairly clear-cut in the *Articles;* the evidence from state practice is even more emphatic. Tams lists 13 instances of states undertaking countermeasures against a state that had violated obligations *erga omnes* between the years 1971 and 2003.[51] Bolstering the evidence from state practice, he produces a pair of statements from international organizations asserting a right to take countermeasures.[52] In terms of the types of violations that have elicited countermeasures, Tams indicates that they have been primarily large-scale violations of human rights obligations or "forcible conduct of another State . . . giving rise to breaches of humanitarian law or causing serious humanitarian concerns . . . at least in the case of systematic or large-scale breaches of international law, there seems to exist a settle practice of countermeasures by States not individually injured."[53] It is worth noting, however, that some of the instances adduced by Tams do not *stricto sensu* constitute countermeasures, because the responding state's action did not constitute a breach of an obligation to the malfeasant state. Technically, that makes these acts of retorsion, which are hostile but always legal, as they do not violate any obligation.[54] Inasmuch as retorsion can be undertaken at any time, those cases do not lend much support to the claim that there is a firm basis in state practice for third states to undertake countermeasures, but on balance the evidence seems to favor the recognition of this right.

To briefly summarize and contextualize the conclusions of the last two sections, although the jurisprudence of the ICJ has indeed recognized that in instances in which an obligation *erga omnes* has been violated, a state not directly affected by the violation may have standing to bring a claim, this allowance is at all times subject to other procedural rules that may prevent the case from being heard irrespective of whether the third state had standing to bring it. With regard to countermeasures, however, there are essentially no obstacles to a state taking direct action to pressure another to cease its violation of an obligation *erga omnes*. Although the use of violence is specifically debarred, this manifestation of the *actio popularis* comes remarkably close to the outlines of classical international punishment. In the concluding section of this chapter, the relationship between *jus cogens* and obligations *erga omnes* will be addressed.

Jus Cogens and Obligations *Erga Omnes*

> To a considerable extent, and almost *per definitionem,* a breach of fundamental rules of international law transcends the usual bilateralism of international relationships.[55]

The final task of this chapter is to delineate the relationship between obligations *erga omnes* and *jus cogens*. It has been widely asserted that the specific obligations *erga omnes* discussed in *Barcelona Traction* were actually *jus cogens*.[56] This has given rise to a great deal of discussion regarding the relationship between the concepts: are *jus cogens* and obligations *erga omnes* necessarily coterminous?[57] Being peremptory characterizes the level of *bindingness* (normativity) of a norm (or its resultant obligation), while operating *erga omnes* characterizes the *scope* of an obligation. "Generality of standing, rather than non-derogable character, is the essence of *erga omnes* rules."[58]

One immediate point of difference is that by definition *jus cogens* cannot be *legitimately* violated, but it is not clear that this is the case with the corpus of obligations *erga omnes*. Additionally, there is no reason that the persistent objector rule, which—as we saw in Chapter 3—is considered inapplicable for *jus cogens* rules, would be inapplicable to an obligation *erga omnes* in formation.[59] As Michael Byers states, "*Jus cogens* rules are necessarily *erga omnes* rules, but . . . *erga omnes* rules could exist which were not of a *jus cogens* character."[60]

I must concur with Byers in his conclusion that if "rules of *jus cogens* necessarily apply *erga omnes*," then rules *erga omnes* definitionally "operate to expand the scope of possible claimants in those situations where traditional rules of standing do not apply suffice." If this is so, then we are led to the conclusion that the violation of *jus cogens* rules should indeed give rise to an *actio popularis*.[61] That said, of course, the caveats illustrated in the present chapter still are to be borne in mind. The simple fact that norms of this type have been violated may indeed give third parties standing, but this does not mean that the ICJ will necessarily be able to hear the case given its own constraining procedural rules. However, as we have seen, the door is open to countermeasures in vindication of violated *jus cogens* rules because of the *erga omnes* obligations they generate.

In the next chapter, the level of analysis changes. Where this chapter was concerned with the universal obligations of *states* and the universal standing of other *states* to take legal action to enforce those obligations, the next looks at the obligations directly binding individual natural persons, and the situations under which *any* state might prosecute them for the violation of those obligations.

CHAPTER 5

The Principle of Universal Jurisdiction

A state has jurisdiction to define and prescribe punishment for certain offenses recognized by the community of nations as of universal concern, such as piracy, slave trade . . . genocide, war crimes . . . even when none of the [traditional] bases of jurisdiction . . . is present . . . Universal jurisdiction over the specified offenses is a result of universal condemnation of these activities and general interest in cooperating to suppress them.[1]

In Chapter 2 we identified the component practices constituting international punishment: a set of nonvoluntary categorical obligations of universal scope and reach, universal interest in compliance with them, and universal standing to enforce compliance or sanction noncompliance. In Chapter 3 we traced the development of a new conceptualization of categorical obligation befitting the modern Positivist-Voluntarist understanding of obligation. In Chapter 4 we analyzed a sort of obligation that while not *in se* peremptory is still universally binding and *ex hypothesi* universally enforceable. Unlike classical punishment, however, these forms of obligation grant at most standing to take legal action and pursue legal vindication of the obligations; they do not entail grounds for the use of force.

In this chapter the level of analysis shifts; in the previous chapter, obligations *erga omnes* and the *actio popularis* to which their violation might in principle give rise were conceptualized in terms of interstate obligations—even if, as in *Barcelona Traction,* the subject matter of the obligations was the treatment of individuals. The obligations treated by international criminal law's Principle of Universal Jurisdiction, while still *generally* peremptory (like those discussed in Chapter 3) and *generally* of universal scope (like those discussed in Chapter 4), bind individuals directly; correspondingly, their violation creates specific individual responsibility. As is the case with interstate obligations *erga omnes,* any state has, *in principle,* the standing to prosecute an accused offender. Indeed, we will see that in particular circumstances, states may be obliged under the principle *aut dedere aut judicare* to either prosecute an accused offender or extradite them for prosecution.[2] Unlike *jus cogens,* obligations *erga omnes,* and the *actio popularis,* universal jurisdiction is explicitly punitive in motivation. As part of international criminal law, the universality principle is oriented toward bringing to justice accused violators of international law's most important rules, ending impunity for perpetrators of these crimes, and *punishing* those found guilty. To a much greater extent than what has been discussed in the preceding two chapters (other than the shift to a focus on individuals), universal jurisdiction mirrors the classical conceptualization of international punishment.

The Principle

Universal jurisdiction competence is just that—universal.[3]

In general, all sources and commentators formulate the underlying idea of universal jurisdiction more or less identically.[4] There are, it is asserted, certain crimes that can be punished by any state without regard to the location of the crime's commission, without regard to the nationality of its perpetrator, and without regard to the nationality of its victims. There is something in the nature of these crimes (and their prohibition) that makes them a matter of concern for all states; "the gravamen of such an offense is that it constitutes a violation against mankind."[5] In other words, the universality principle grants jurisdiction even in the absence of the other, traditional forms of jurisdiction.

Generally, for a state to exercise criminal jurisdiction over a person (whether natural or juridical) there must be either a territorial link, a relation of nationality, or a directly affected state interest. The Territorial Principle addresses states' jurisdiction over crimes committed in their territory. The Nationality Principle concerns states' jurisdiction over their nationals, wherever they may be. Its obverse, the Passive Personality Principle, grants states jurisdiction over those who harm their nationals. Because harm to a national that occurs within the state's territory falls under the Territorial Principle, the main focus of the Passive Personality Principle is extraterritorial jurisdiction. This principle has generated significant controversy.[6] Finally, the Protective Principle, also primarily oriented toward extraterritorial application, grants jurisdiction over parties engaging in acts that harm the state's essential interests.

In each of the preceding bases of jurisdiction there must be a material link between the state asserting jurisdiction and the crime. That is what distinguishes the Universality Principle from the other bases; there need not be *any* specific link between the crime, its perpetrator or victims, and the state undertaking to exercise jurisdiction.[7] The often-made comparison with the *actio popularis* appears on the face of things to be quite apt; universal jurisdiction entails prosecution undertaken in the public interest. "The exercising state acts on behalf of the international community because it has an interest in the preservation of world order as a member of that community.... [It is] a surrogate for the international community."[8] This is not to say that there is anything more than an analogy between the two practices.[9] The basis of the analogy is the oft-made assertion that crimes *jure gentium*—beyond being crimes against their immediate, material victims—are crimes against the entire international community, or the interests of the international community. It is because of this that any member of the community can take legal action against the violator; hence, the analogy to the *actio popularis*.

> Crimes under international law are directed against the interests of the international community as a whole. It follows from this universal nature of international crimes that the international community is empowered to prosecute and punish these crimes, regardless of who committed them or against whom they were committed. Every legal system may defend itself

> with criminal sanctions against attacks on its elementary values... The authority to punish derives from the crime itself.[10]

The universality principle has generated a great deal of controversy, in equal parts exegetical and political. Although the political issues are to a degree inseparable and will be treated in this chapter's discussions of *Eichmann, Pinochet,* and *Congo v Belgium* (and Belgium's universal jurisdiction legislation underlying it), the chapter will focus on the conceptual issues related to universality and the linkages to international punishment. Before turning to the guiding concern with how to explain the assertion of universality in a particularistic Positivist legal framework, the next step must be to trace the development of the idea and practice of universal jurisdiction.

Piracy

> The crime of piracy, or robbery and depredation on the high seas, is an offence against the universal law of society; a pirate being... *hostis humani generis.* As therefore he has renounced all the benefits of society and government, and has reduced himself... to the savage state of nature, by declaring war against all mankind, all mankind must declare war against him: so that every community hath a right, by the rule of self-defence, to inflict that punishment on him, which every individual would in a state of nature have been otherwise entitled to do.[11]

Although the authors of Amnesty International's 2001 Document on Universal Jurisdiction follow Henri Donnedieu de Vabres (the main French judge at Nuremberg) in finding a (rather tenuous) precursor to our understanding of universal jurisdiction in the fourth-century Code of Justinian,[12] it is canonical to trace current practice to the reaction of the early modern state system to piracy (and its terrestrial counterpart, brigandage).[13] The most commonly asserted basis for the customary law status of exercising universal jurisdiction over some criminals is that pirates have been historically regarded as *hostes humani generis,* enemies of all humankind.[14] As *hostes humani generis* (sometimes rendered *hostes omnium*)[15] they were universally condemned and the targets of widespread suppression (extermination) efforts—taking in particular the form of any state trying and punishing pirates.[16] "All nations are engaged in a league against [pirates] for the mutual defense and safety of all."[17]

> A pirate is deemed, and properly deemed, *hostis humani generis*. But why is he so deemed? Because he commits hostilities upon the subjects and property of any or all nations, without any regard to right or duty, or any pretense of public authority. If he willfully sinks or destroys an innocent merchant ship, without any other object than to gratify his lawless appetite for mischief, it is just as much a piratical aggression, in the sense of the law of nations, and of the act of Congress, as if he did it solely and exclusively for the sake of plunder, *lucri causa*. The law looks to it as an act of hostility, and being committed by a vessel not commissioned and engaged in lawful warfare, it treats it as the act of a pirate, and of one who is emphatically *hostis humani generis*.[18]

This, it is usually claimed, established a precedent of long standing (allegedly predating our modern understanding of international law) for doing the same with crimes that have subsequently been analogized with piracy, from the slave trade to hijacking, torture, and genocide.[19] Perhaps not ever explicitly formulated in today's terms, the suppression of piracy is claimed to have borne all of the hallmarks of our contemporary understanding of universal jurisdiction: "Every state has long had legislative, adjudicatory and enforcement jurisdiction over all piratical acts on the high seas, even when neither the pirates nor the victims are nationals of the prosecuting state and the offense has no specific connection to the prosecuting state."[20] Coming from uncoordinated state practice, the result was a customary law basis for universal jurisdiction over pirates that was subsequently formalized in a number of treaties.[21] Prominent among these treaties are Articles 14–21 of the 1958 *Geneva Convention on the Law of the High Seas* and Articles 100–107 of the 1987 *United Nations Convention on the Law of the Seas*—which have converted standing to prosecute and punish to a formal obligation of the *aut dedere aut judicare* character.[22]

Several possible reasons have been adduced for pirates having been considered *hostes humani generis*. Kenneth Randall and Yana Shy Kraytman prefer economic explanations: "The practice evolved from the importance placed upon naval trade and communication links between states, which were constantly and indiscriminately threatened by piracy."[23] Under this theory, pirates interfered with a key (economic) interest of all humanity that made them the enemies of all humanity; so all humanity shared an interest in their suppression, and all states had the standing to do so.

The authors of the Amnesty International report incline toward a functional explanation: piracy occurs outside of any state's jurisdiction, therefore any state must be able to punish piracy or it would necessarily go unpunished.[24] This interpretation seems to cast them less as enemies of all than as simple criminals that any party might try given the geography of their criminal activity. Their reading, however, ignores the other jurisdictional bases that still operated regardless of the geographic setting of piracy: the state in which accosted the ship was registered still had territorial jurisdiction, the home state of the victims of piracy still had passive personality jurisdiction, and the home state of the pirates themselves still had nationality jurisdiction. It was not the case of an *absence* of other jurisdictional bases simply because the crimes occurred on the high seas, although the logistics of exercising jurisdiction were immensely complicated.[25]

Others focus on the "heinous" character of piracy: "Piracy often consists of heinous acts of violence or depredation, which are committed indiscriminately against the vessels and nationals of numerous states."[26] This "heinousness" became the crux of the analogy between piracy and the other crimes of universal jurisdiction. When slavery, genocide, war crimes, crimes against humanity, the "gravest crimes," the crimes that "shock the conscience of nations," the crimes that "sicken the conscience of civilized humanity.... [and] are ... universally abhorrent"[27] are analogized to the wickedness of piracy, we find conclusions such as the following: "Some crimes are so heinous that they offend the interest of all humanity—indeed, they imperil civilization itself" justifying the assertion of universality of jurisdiction.[28] While economic or functional rationales may be more empirically accurate—in either isolation or aggregate—this explanation is the one that has been most widely seized upon in the subsequent development of universal jurisdiction. The account that has been offered by most advocates of universal jurisdiction is that pirates were the subjects of any state's criminal jurisdiction because of the *character* of their acts, and likewise any parties that commit outrages of similar turpitude are also rightly subject to the criminal jurisdiction of any state. Eugene Kontorovich reminds us that the "seminal cases that helped expand universal jurisdiction to new offenses...have *all* used the piracy analogy."[29] Hence, Justice Jackson's statement at *Nuremberg:* "The principle of individual responsibility for piracy and brigandage, which have long been recognized as crimes punishable under international law, is old and well established. That is what illegal warfare is."[30] Hence also, the 2nd Circuit's 1980 appellate holding in *Filartiga:* "The torturer has become—like the pirate and the slave trader before him—*hostis humani generis,* an enemy of all mankind."[31]

Despite the weight of repetition, the link between the heinousness of piracy and the heinousness of "modern" crimes of universal jurisdiction is still subject to a strain of criticism about the validity of the underlying analogy.[32] The strongest critics are undoubtedly Kontorovich and Alfred Rubin. They make a number of powerful points; one of the most damning is the empirical question of whether piracy was actually considered "heinous" during the time in which the custom is canonically understood to have been in formation. If it were indeed a universally condemned practice, why was it also a *state-sanctioned* practice?[33] Article 1, Section 8, of the U.S. Constitution still contains provision for the commissioning of privateers.[34] Piracy, from the ancient world to UNCLOS, has been defined as robbery committed on the high seas. Apparently there is robbery, and then there is robbery. Robbery committed on the high seas *with* state sanction is not criminal.[35] Privateers engaged in the identical set of practices as pirates, including killing, mutilations, and "outrages against women"—indeed the same individuals often played both roles at various times—but privateering was never denounced as "heinous" or "outrageous." If two practices are distinguishable only *in nomine* and with regard to state sanction (one is reminded of Hobbes's comments on superstition and religion),[36] how can one of them be "heinous" or "revolting" and the other perfectly respectable?[37] What could be so intrinsically wrong about piracy that could still be wiped away merely by state sanction? If we accept that state sanction can expunge the repugnance of what we are told is the worst crime, what then is to keep this from being applied to *inter alia* state-sponsored genocide?

It is not clear from the records of contemporary court cases whether piracy was even considered a crime of any special gravity. Rubin and Kontorovich's respective surveys of the case law indicate that piracy was regarded as no worse a crime than ordinary, terrestrial robbery, and less serious than murder. Conversely, crimes that were regarded as *worse* than piracy were not held to give rise to universal jurisdiction.[38] Both Kontorovich and Rubin demonstrate that during the period of the purported formation of the custom, there is a paucity of evidence of piracy prosecutions undertaken on the basis of a jurisdictional claim other than the ordinary bases, and that at least one state explicitly denied its courts universal jurisdiction over piracy.[39]

While Kontorovich and Rubin are plainly correct on empirical and analytic grounds, they miss an important point: regardless of the aptness of the analogy, regardless of whether pirates were actually considered *hostes humani generis* during the formative period of the rule (or indeed prior), regardless of whether their crimes were considered heinous, regardless of whether states were actually exercising jurisdiction over a crime *jure gentium,* rather than exercising extraordinary jurisdiction in trying and punishing them, the analogy *was* indeed drawn, and the emphasis *was* placed on creating universal jurisdiction over crimes considered especially heinous. The analogy was drawn repeatedly; successive cases systematically cited previous invocations of the *hostis humani* formulation, those courts invoking it themselves and repeating the mistake, but thereby actually *creating* the custom they believed themselves to be *applying.* The analogy, robust or flawed, was utilized to *create* a new form of jurisdiction. The references to the classical world and to Renaissance and early modern sources may be misplaced, but international society has created a category for crimes it considers to be the gravest, and has done so on the basis of, in part, this flawed analogy. It is a well-known (if not universally subscribed) view in international law that all customary international law rests ultimately upon factual mistakes—Byers calls this the "chronological paradox"; Jörg Kammerhofer calls it the *"opinio juris* paradox"—"States creating new customary rules must believe that those rules already exist, and that their practice, therefore, *is* in accordance with the law . . . the relevant actors must *erroneously* believe that they are already bound by that rule."[40] Surely, what holds with mistaken assertions of fact holds as well with mistaken analogies.

The Slave Trade

Leaving piracy behind, the next step in the canonical account of the development of universal jurisdiction was the suppression of the international slave trade. Piracy is not left far behind, however; there are a number of instances in which explicit analogy was made between the slave trade and piracy as part of the effort to mobilize support for the suppression of the former.[41] As I alluded to in the previous discussion, the crux of the analogy was that "like piracy, both the slave trade and slavery were considered as particularly atrocious crimes."[42] Some treaties, notably the 1815 *Declaration of the Congress of Vienna,* the 1822 *Declaration of the Congress of Verona,* and Article One of the 1841 *Treaty for the Suppression of the African Slave Trade* (Austria, France, the United Kingdom, Prussia, Russia)—also known as the *London Treaty*—moved beyond analogy to equation, and asserted that the slave trade was actually piracy *simpliciter.*[43]

The path to universal jurisdiction over the slave trade, however, was significantly different from that taken by piracy; rather than starting from uncoordinated state practice and (arguably) evolving into a customary rule, the drive to suppress the slave trade and to create universal jurisdiction over those who engaged in it was treaty driven from the outset. Deriving from bilateral and narrowly multilateral treaties, however, the prohibition could not have been universal originally because a fundamental principle of treaty law, *pacta tertiis nec nocent nec prosunt,* limits obligations arising from treaties solely to parties thereto.[44] Unlike piracy, over which there was by this point at least arguably universal jurisdiction, the enforcement mechanism contained in the *London Treaty* and its successors, including the 1862 *Treaty for the Suppression of the Slave Trade* (the United States-the United Kingdom), could create jurisdiction *only* among parties. Kontorovich is particularly insistent on this point: "The use of formal treaties shows that international custom did not recognize a right of third-party nations to prosecute slave traders."[45] He might well have added that not only did it not create third party rights, but also it created neither third party obligations nor party rights over nonparty ships. Rather than universal jurisdiction *per se,* these treaties created a sphere of shared jurisdiction.[46] They provided for joint policing of clearly delineated areas of the Atlantic (primarily the coasts of Africa and Cuba), and allowed naval vessels of parties to board; search; and, if evidence of participation in the trade was found, detain (only) the merchant ships of other parties. In case of detention, the procedures varied between treaties; Article VII of the 1841 *London Treaty* stipulated that the detained ship and its crew would be taken to a port of their home state for trial; Article IV of the 1862 U.S.-UK treaty called for the creation of three mixed Tribunals—in New York, Sierra Leone, and the Cape of Good Hope—for accused slave traders.[47]

It is M. Cherif Bassiouni's assertion that the *London Treaty* effectively criminalized the slave trade first by equating it with piracy, which by this point was widely accepted as criminal, and second by prescribing the *aut dedere* rule.[48] Fischer disagrees: "The mere engagement of the Powers to declare the slave-trade to be piracy, and even the fulfillment of this engagement did not make it [criminal] *jure gentium.*"[49] Bassiouni is mistaken on another point; there is no basis to infer the existence—even implicitly—of the *aut dedere* obligation in these treaties. At no point in either document's respective treatment of search and seizure is the language imperative in mood; rather they consistently use the modal "may." It is no more credible to infer an obligation from a permissive (a "must" from a "may") than an "ought" from an "is"—at least until that "may" has become normativized by the process of customary law formation.[50]

The place of the suppression of the slave trade in the evolution of universal jurisdiction is even less clear than that of the suppression of piracy. Because it was initially treaty based, jurisdiction over slave traders could not have become universal in any meaningful sense prior to the prohibition becoming part of customary law, and prior to the actual exercise of jurisdiction becoming sufficiently widespread and sufficiently widely accepted as to have become part of customary law. Kontorovich sees no basis for such development in any of the treaties discussed, "since none of the treaties provided for universal jurisdiction, they could hardly be the germ of such a custom."[51] The situation with regard to the slave trade might be read as similar to that of piracy: the repeated, successful (albeit mistaken) assertion of jurisdiction over slave traders in the belief that jurisdiction was universal is perhaps what has created universal jurisdiction. We also find the assertion offered that the *jus cogens* character of the prohibition of slavery creates universal jurisdiction.[52] As we saw in chapters 2 and 3, however, there is no automatic link between the categorical character of a rule's obligation and universality to enforce it.

Analysis of the current state of international human rights law and international criminal law, however, indicates that this is an area in which jurisdiction is still primarily treaty derived. No treaty dealing with the subject offers a clear assertion of universal jurisdiction. Although there is no clear evidence in the form of treaty law or judicial findings that universal jurisdiction is accepted as matter of customary law, §404 of the *Restatement 3rd* does include slavery among crimes subject to universal jurisdiction,[53] and ICJ justice Rosalyn Higgins believes that universal jurisdiction over the slave trade is quite plainly established.[54] For Bassiouni, when viewed in their totality, the treaties addressing slavery—in particular the raft of twentieth-century treaties—sum to evidence of a customary rule.[55] Max Sorensen cautiously shares this assessment: "In view of the extensive treaties seeking to wipe out slave-trade, it is *possible* that international customary law would today sustain an assertion of universal jurisdiction with respect to this offense."[56] One area in which slavery is unquestionably subject to universal jurisdiction is when committed during time of war, constituting in such a situation a war crime.

War Crimes and Crimes Against Humanity

While piracy and the slave trade are *largely* historical issues, or were thought so prior to the explosion in pirate activity off the East African coast, the areas most commonly associated with universal jurisdiction are regrettably very live issues. The paradigm international crimes—war crimes, crimes against humanity, and genocide—are all subject to universal jurisdiction. Rather than engage in yet another lengthy history of the development of jurisdiction over these crimes, we now turn to analysis of particular exemplary episodes.[57]

The canonical twentieth-century starting points, the post-World War Two prosecutions, are regrettably every bit as controversial as what we have seen so far.[58] The question of whether the courts in *inter alia* Nuremberg and Tokyo were exercising universal jurisdiction or a more quotidian jurisdictional basis is still disputed. The dispute lingers in no small part because of inconsistencies in the way in which the Tribunals' jurisdictional bases were articulated in their constitutive instruments and across various decisions.

There are actually very few advocates of the view that the primary Tribunals operated on the basis of universal jurisdiction. Amnesty International remains the strongest advocate of this view; the lynchpin of its position, indeed that of most advocates of this view, is a widely quoted passage:

> The Signatory Powers created this Tribunal, defined the law it was to administer, and made regulations for the proper conduct of the Trial. *In doing so, they have done together what any one of them might have done singly; for it is not to be doubted that any nation has the right thus to set up special courts to administer law.*[59]

In isolation, this appears to be a clear assertion of universal jurisdiction; however, making overly bold claims on the basis of only this passage is untenable. The authors of the Amnesty International report elide the context of those two sentences.[60] The first paragraph roots the Tribunal's jurisdiction in "the [London] Agreement and Charter [of the International Military Tribunal]." The second paragraph gives a nationality principle basis to the Tribunal's decision, stating, "The making of the Charter was the exercise of sovereign legislative power by the countries to which the German Reich unconditionally surrendered; and the undoubted right of these countries to legislate for the occupied territories has been recognized by the civilized world."[61] *At most,* this quotation can be read as asserting an ancillary role for universal jurisdiction, but even here, such a claim is perilous given the absence of universalist language anywhere else in either the Agreement or the Charter.

The more common position is that regardless of whether universality was a conceivable basis of jurisdiction, it was not a necessary basis for the International Military Tribunal; "the prosecuting states had no need to raise the universality principle if they had a specific connection with an offense."[62] Consider the other jurisdictional bases: if a state's nationals were victims of Nazi crimes, the Passive Personality Principle was operative; if a state had been occupied by the Nazis, the Territorial Principle provided a jurisdictional basis. In cases for which one of these links did not apply, cases in which the crimes being prosecuted were committed in another state's territory against another state's nationals, crimes with which the prosecuting state had no material link, as the then recognized sovereign powers in Germany, they had (as indicated in the previously quoted second paragraph of the decision) nationality jurisdiction over the accused.[63] This, however, does not reflect the ways in which jurisdiction was justified in all of the prosecutions undertaken after the end of the war.

The Nuremberg proceedings against the "Major War Criminals" can be explained by these ordinary bases of jurisdiction, but some of the later, "Zonal" prosecutions undertaken pursuant to *Allied Control Council Law Number Ten* do not fit within this schema; in these cases, there is at least a case to be made that universal jurisdiction was being exercised. A brief survey will prove instructive.

The best known of these cases is the American-prosecuted *List* case (also referred to as the *Hostages Case*). In this case, German officers were put on trial for crimes committed in Greece and the Balkans. There was no passive personality jurisdiction for the United States to assert, and rather than rely on America's jurisdiction as the *de facto* sovereigns over their zone of Germany, the court chose to emphasize the universal character of both the crimes with which the accused were charged (the massacres of hostages) and the jurisdiction arising from them. The Tribunal asserted that these massacres constituted international crimes, and that crimes of that category were universally cognizable; those accused of their commission were therefore "subject to the authority of any state that captured them."[64] We find similar interpretations and assertions by the British in *Almelo*,[65] and *Zyklon B*,[66] by the United States in *Hadamar*[67] and in *re Eisentrager*,[68] and by the French in *Monte*.[69] In each of these cases the prosecuting state could (and in some instances did) base the court's jurisdiction on nationality or passive personality, but in each instance, that was not the primary emphasis; rather the focus was on the universal character of the crime. Although these cases are widely cited as marking strong moves toward universal jurisdiction over war crimes and crimes against humanity, advocates elide the point that these cases' jurisdictional statements are in no way representative of the larger body of post-World War Two case law, and signify a very small percentage of the trials conducted.

Adolf Eichmann

We find a clearer, more defensible—if not universally accepted—instance of the Universality Principle in operation in *Eichmann*.[70] Here too, a great deal of weight is placed upon the piracy analogy; §13 of the Jerusalem District Court's decision invoked a familiar litany of sources to illustrate the pedigree of the idea of universal jurisdiction over pirates, and thus the customary law status of the rule allowing it.[71] This approach was mirrored in §11(1) of the Israeli Supreme Court's Appeal Judgment.[72] Treating universal jurisdiction over pirates as well established, both bodies then took the familiar step of analogizing modern international crimes with piracy, and documenting the evidence for their acceptance as crimes of universal jurisdiction to defend Israel's jurisdiction from the objections raised by Eichmann's defense counsel. Leaving aside the question of the legitimacy of Eichmann's kidnapping from Argentina, questions were raised about Israel's standing to try crimes that did not take place on its territory, and were neither committed by nor against its nationals.

The primary basis of their assertion of jurisdiction was the 1950 *Nazis and Nazi Collaborators (Punishment) Law*, which stipulated that commission of Crimes Against the Jewish People, Crimes Against Humanity, or War Crimes "during the period of the Nazi regime, in an enemy country" was punishable by death.[73] The law was obviously constructed to have extraterritorial effect. In response to the assertion that this legislation was in violation of international law, both courts went to great pains to demonstrate its conformity with the evolving understanding of universal jurisdiction. The District Court emphasized the "universal character of the crimes in question," that the crimes were "grave offences against the law of nations itself (*delicta juris gentium*)," and ultimately that "the jurisdiction to try crimes under international law is universal."[74] In support of this line of argumentation, the Court turned to *Nuremberg* and the Zonal prosecutions as precedents. Bolstering the authority of these decisions, the Court also cited the more recent UN General Assembly 1946 *Resolution on the Crime of Genocide*, the 1948 *Convention on the Prevention and Punishment of the Crime of Genocide*, and the ICJ's 1950/51 *Advisory Opinion on Reservations to the Convention on the Prevention and Punishment of the Crime of Genocide* as all clearly asserting that the crimes with which

Eichmann was accused were international crimes and could thus by definition be punished by any state.

The Israeli Supreme Court followed a similar line of reasoning, asserting:

> The crimes created by the Law and of which the Appellant was convicted must be deemed today to have always borne the stamp of international crimes, banned by international law and entailing individual criminal liability; it is the particular universal character of these crimes that vests in each state the power to try and punish any one who assisted in their commission . . . [These crimes] constitute acts which damage vital international interests; they impair the foundations and security of the international community; they violate universal moral values and humanitarian principles . . . The underlying principle in international law that governs such crimes is that the individual who has committed any of them . . . must account in law for his behaviour . . . it is the universal character of the crimes in question which vests in every state the power to try those who participated in the perpetration of such crimes and to punish them.[75]

It was to provide support for these expansive claims that the two courts turned to the piracy analogy.

It is Randall's conclusion that this case represents the strongest articulation of the universality principle of the post-World War Two trials.[76] Kontorovich, however, focuses upon the language of "Crimes Against the Jewish People" to assert that this was not a universal jurisdiction-based trial, but rather a simpler instance of passive personality jurisdiction. Kontorovich's general skepticism notwithstanding, both courts' insistence that the category "Crimes Against the Jewish People" was an instance of Genocide and a species of Crimes Against Humanity, and that "all that has been said in the Nuremberg principles on the 'crimes against humanity' applies *a fortiori* to the 'crime against the Jewish People'" bears emphasizing.[77] While making this claim, and insisting that this (putative) assertion of universal jurisdiction is as hamstrung as its predecessors by its reliance on the flawed piracy analogy, Kontorovich emphasizes that ultimately Israel need not have turned to universality, already having a firm jurisdictional claim.[78]

Augusto Pinochet

Eichmann was the trial of a functionary, an instrumental one admittedly; the extradition proceedings in England against Augusto Pinochet held pursuant to Spain's two international arrest warrants marked the first instance of an attempted exercise of universal jurisdiction by one state against a former head of state.[79] The case is divided into three phases (following the convention of *Pinochet I, II,* and *III*); the first and third of which dealt with the issue of whether Pinochet, as a former head of state, was subject to foreign jurisdiction and hence amenable to extradition.[80] In both proceedings the majority of the Law Lords held that Pinochet was not immune; the findings of the first proceeding were set aside because of the appearance of conflict of interest, requiring the matter to be heard again (the decision to set aside was the subject matter of *Pinochet II*).

The line of reasoning in both decisions is broadly the same. If Pinochet were still the Chilean head of state, he would have complete immunity *ratione personae* (personal immunity), and British courts would be unable to proceed against him. As a former head of state, however, he lost this form of immunity upon stepping down. His legal team stipulated to this conclusion, but argued that while he could no longer avail himself of the immunity that attaches to the office, he still possessed immunity *ratione materiae* (functional immunity) for any acts done while in office *in his official capacity.*

The fundamental question became whether the crimes with which the Spanish court had accused Pinochet were of such a character that immunity would not attach. As framed by a number of the Lords, the defining issue was whether acts that were specifically identified as international crimes in both customary and conventional law, and were explicitly recognized as such by the government of Chile, might be construed for legal purposes as official acts of office. Because of the particularities of British legislation, a number of the charges for which Spain sought Pinochet's extradition were judged for various reasons to be nonextraditable; the primary charge that remained was torture and conspiracy to torture.[81] The fundamental issue for decision was thus whether torture could be construed as an official function of office; was torture, which had been recognized as an international crime by Chile when Pinochet was in fact still in office an official function of his office? If torture in contravention of Chile's international legal obligations was a function of Pinochet's office, he would be protected by immunity *ratione materiae;* if it was not found to be an official function, he would not be immune, and would be legally able to be extradited to Spain; "the concept of an individual performing the functions of head of state implied that there are actions not included with such functions. A meaningful line had to be drawn."[82]

In the event, none of the Lords even approached the assertion that torture might be an official role of office, although a lower court had reached that conclusion, leading Lord Steyn to conclude of their decision: "It follows [from the lower court's decision] that when Hitler ordered the 'final solution' his act must be regarded as an official act deriving from the exercise of his functions a Head of State. This is where the reason of the Divisional Court inexorably leads."[83]

The majority of both *Pinochet I* and *III* held that while criminal immunity attached to ordinary crimes of domestic law, it could not attach to international crimes, particularly as the *Torture Convention* had been formulated. One cannot commit torture in violation of international law while acting *qua* president.[84] "It hardly needs saying that torture . . . would not be regarded by international law as a function of a head of state. All states disavow the use of torture as abhorrent . . . international law has made plain that certain types of conduct . . . are not acceptable conduct on the part of anyone. This applies as much to heads of state, or even more so, as it does to everyone else."[85]

Lord Browne-Wilkinson brought this line of reasoning and the consequences of its rejection into sharper focus in his opinion in *Pinochet III.*

> Can it be said that the commission of a crime which is an international crime against humanity and *jus cogens* is an act done in official capacity on behalf of a state? I believe there to be strong ground for saying that the

> implementation of torture as defined by the Torture Convention cannot be a state function . . . [The Torture Convention] required all member states to ban and outlaw torture. How can it be for international law purposes an official function to do something which international law itself prohibits and criminalises . . . if the implementation of a torture regime is a public function giving rise to immunity *ratione materiae,* this produces bizarre results. Immunity *ratione materiae* applies not only to ex-heads of state . . . but to all state officials who have been involved in carrying out the functions of the state . . . if the implementation of the torture regime is to be treated as official business sufficient to found an immunity for the former head of state, it must also be official business sufficient to justify immunity for his inferiors who actually did the torturing.[86]

Article 1(1) of the *Torture Convention* had defined torture in terms of acts committed "by or at the instigation of or with the consent or acquiescence of a public official"; for Lord Millett, this was pivotal.

> The offence can be committed *only* by or at the instigation of or with the consent or acquiescence of a public official . . . The official or governmental nature of the act, which forms the basis of the immunity, is an essential ingredient of the offence. No rational system of criminal justice can allow an immunity which is co-extensive with the offence . . . The offence is one which could only be committed in circumstances which would normally give rise to . . . immunity. The international community had created an offence for which immunity *ratione materiae* could not possibly be available. International law cannot be supposed to have established a crime having the character of a *jus cogens* and at the same time to have provided and immunity with is co-extensive with the obligation it seeks to impose.[87]

Some assertions by a subset of the majority notwithstanding, *Pinochet* does not represent a strong articulation of universal jurisdiction.[88] Although some of the Lords emphasized an underlying, antecedent jurisdictional basis from customary law, and the *amicus* brief from Amnesty International sought to frame things in part in terms of abstract notions of universal jurisdiction, the consensus position based jurisdiction in *aut dedere aut judicare* obligations from the *Torture Convention* and more immediately from the acts of British legislation adopting the treaty obligations. "They talked about universal jurisdiction, but grounded their decision in domestic statutory law."[89] This was a matter ultimately of *inter partes* obligation arising from a treaty to which the three relevant states were parties.[90] Had a nonparty state sought extradition from the UK bases solely on a claim of universal jurisdiction over the crime of torture, it seems clear that the court would have been bound to reject it.

Congo v. Belgium

If the trajectory from the assertion of universal jurisdiction over pirates to *Pinochet* gave the appearance of linear progression, hopes for the consolidation of the practice were set back by the ICJ's decision in *Congo v Belgium,* and in the subsequent modifications and ultimate neutering of Belgium's universal jurisdiction law. In 1993 Belgium passed an ambitious piece of legislation that represented an attempt to exercise "absolute universal jurisdiction."[91] It gave Belgium's national courts jurisdiction over international crimes (initially war crimes, later amended to countenance crimes against humanity and genocide) in cases in which there need be no other, more traditional jurisdictional nexus. In fact, it did not even require the presence of the accused in Belgium, allowing for issuance of international arrest warrants. This last provision was held to be an overreach. Defeated at the ICJ when one of these arrest warrants was challenged,[92] and threatened by other states if Belgium were to pursue prosecutions under this legislation, it was repeatedly weakened until it scarcely carried an element of universal jurisdiction.[93]

As originally formulated, Belgium's 1993 law addressed jurisdictional issues in Articles 5 (3) and 7(1). "Article 5(3) originally provided that 'the Act shall apply equally to all persons without any distinction based on official capacity ... Article 7(1) provided 'Belgian courts are competent to take cognizance of offences stipulated in the present law irrespective of the place where they have been committed.' "[94] Belgian domestic courts thus were granted the right to try crimes that had no traditional jurisdictional link to Belgium. Article 5(3), following a pattern familiar since Nuremberg, refused to grant immunity on the basis of the office held by the accused. The 1999 amendment clarified the interpretation of the denial of immunity, holding "the immunity attributed to the official capacity of a person does not prevent the application of the present act."[95] In a case brought against Ariel Sharon under this law, however, a Belgian court did uphold the customary law-based immunity for incumbent office holders—a position affirmed in Pinochet, and largely uncontroversial.[96]

A unique feature of this legislation, Article 9(3) granted victims of these crimes present in Belgium the standing to initiate proceedings in Belgian courts through a procedure known as *constitution de partie civile*. Although they cannot "bring prosecutions before the courts ... they may initiate a criminal investigation" and irrespective of the action of the prosecutor's office, bring the matter to an "examining magistrate." Once the magistrate has been seized of the matter, the court is required to investigate, and the government may not prevent the investigation from proceeding.[97]

Examining the records of parliamentary debate, Luc Reydams concludes that it was "the drafters' intent that the law be enforced even when a suspect is not found or present in Belgium. ... a foreign accused can be prosecuted or tried in Belgium after being extradited from abroad, or even *in absentia* when extradition is impossible."[98] The inclusion of provision for prosecution after extradition is perfectly commonplace, and an outgrowth of the *aut dedere* provisions in the treaties to which Belgium was party. Assertion of the right to trial *in absentia* was rather bolder.

In April 2000, a Belgian court issued an arrest warrant for the then foreign minister of the Democratic Republic of the Congo, Abdulaye Yerodia Ndombasi, alleging that before taking office he had been involved in crimes against humanity and war crimes. Specifically, he was alleged to have incited a campaign of ethnic violence against Tutsis in the Congo, "resulting in several hundred deaths and in summary executions, arbitrary arrests, lynchings, and unfair trials."[99] The Congolese government challenged the validity of this arrest warrant, asserting that Belgium was attempting to unlawfully exercise its authority on the sovereign territory of the DRC, violating the "principle of sovereign equality among all Members of the United Nations" and violating Minister Yerodia's diplomatic immunity.[100] Although the first of these grounds was a direct challenge to Belgium's assertion of universal jurisdiction in its 1993/1999 legislation, Congo discontinued that part of its claim, focusing only on the issue of Belgium violating Yerodia's immunity.[101] Under the rules of the Court, although discussion of immunity logically presupposes the question of jurisdiction, because of Congo's discontinuation, the ICJ could not directly address the universal jurisdiction issue.[102]

Because the ICJ was limited to the immunity issue, it was faced with a series of questions related to the scope of the immunities of a foreign minister and possible derogations from them. *Pinochet* seemed to make clear that although incumbent *heads of state* could not be prosecuted, upon leaving office they could be prosecuted for internationally criminalized acts. Congo shared this understanding of head of state immunity, but claimed that absolute immunity *ratione materiae* extended as well to incumbent *foreign ministers*. Belgium's reasoning went in the opposite direction, arguing that the immunity *ratione personae* of foreign ministers did not extend to international crimes, and ended completely upon loss of office.

The Court agreed with the Congo on the implicit equation of head of state immunity with that of foreign ministers and thus that incumbent immunity was absolute—rejecting for these purposes the distinction Belgium asserted between acts taken in an official capacity and those not so taken. "The Court . . . concludes that the functions of a Minister of Foreign Affairs are such that, throughout the duration of his or her office, he or she . . . enjoys full immunity from criminal jurisdiction and inviolability."[103] Most significantly, the Court found no exceptions to this rule for commission of war crimes and crimes against humanity.

Superficially in line with *Pinochet,* the Court did hold that some immunities cease when the official leaves office. However, the specified immunities did not extend to international crimes committed while in office:

> After a person ceases to hold the office of Minister of Foreign Affairs, he
> or she will no longer enjoy all of the immunities accorded by international
> law . . . a court of one State may try a former Minister for Foreign Affairs
> of another state *in respect of acts committed prior or subsequent to his or her
> period of office, as well as in respect of acts committed during that period of
> office in a private capacity.*[104]

This was one of the four ways that the Court sought to demonstrate that the immunity it upheld for Yerodia did not amount to impunity. The others were trial in the home state of the accused, waiver of immunity by the accused's home state, and trial before an international tribunal with specific jurisdiction.

There is much to be dissatisfied about in the decision the ICJ rendered. Much of it is reflected in the Separate and Dissenting Opinions. A number of judges were uncomfortable with the Court addressing immunity in isolation from the jurisdiction from which Congo was claiming immunity: President Guillaume indicated this in the opinion he appended.[105] The Joint Separate Opinion of judges Higgins, Kooijmans, and Buergenthal stated the issue far more emphatically.[106] This dissatisfaction is shared in the literature.[107]

The missed opportunity to render an opinion on universal jurisdiction is regrettable but not altogether surprising; the Court's stance on immunity is lamentable both normatively and doctrinally. To briefly summarize what it articulated, a foreign minister's immunity *ratione personae* is fully coextensive with that of a head of state—it is, in other words, absolute. The Court found no evidence of *any* exception to this principle.[108] Further, the ICJ held that a former foreign minister's immunity *ratione materiae* is likewise absolute; any act undertaken in an official capacity—which it understood to be any act not wholly personal in character—carries with it absolute immunity. By the logic of this decision, no international crime committed by a foreign minister, and *a fortiori* by a head of state (and presumably head of government) can ever be prosecuted by a foreign court. Yet this is alleged to not be *impunity* because they might be prosecuted by their home state, have their immunity waived, or be prosecuted by an international tribunal. This claim was rightly greeted with both incredulity and derision. The "recognition" of absolute immunity *ratione personae* has been ably demonstrated to fly in the face of existing treaty and case law.[109] Insisting on complete immunity *ratione materiae* is an outright contradiction of every development since Nuremberg, including the constitutive instrument of the ICJ's very neighbor, the International Criminal Court.

Conceptualizing Universality in a Positivist-Voluntarist Setting

By tracing the history of Universal Jurisdiction from the suppression of piracy to the ICJ's decision in *Congo,* a broad stroke answer to the question of how to conceptualize universals in a particularistic, Voluntarist environment begins to take shape. There are two notions of universality at play in this discussion: universality of obligation and universality of enforcement. Although they are conceptually distinct, they are obviously linked: the latter cannot easily be asserted in the absence of the former. What seems to be at stake in discussion of universal jurisdiction is universal standing to enforce universal obligations, or to use the language of an earlier chapter, the right *erga omnes* to enforce an obligation *erga omnes,* which brings us right back to the discussion at the chapter's beginning of the parallels between universal jurisdiction and the *actio populialis*.

To cut into this problem, it is necessary to return to the question of universal obligation albeit in a manner somewhat different from that of Chapter 3. Doctrinally, there are two simple ways that obligations of universal scope might come about; the first is with the creation of a treaty with universal membership. Under current rules, such a treaty will, strictly speaking, only create *inter partes* obligation, but since the set of parties is equal to the set of all states, it is universal in at least a nominal, superficial sense. No such treaties yet exist, and as we will see, universality of membership and obligation does not *ipso facto* yield universal standing to vindicate breached obligations.

Still trying to resolve this problem in Positivist terms, the other doctrinally straightforward place to look for universal obligation is customary law. As custom does not require explicit consent, but only practice and silence—which is interpreted as acquiescence, or, less felicitously, "implied consent"—it is easily conceivable that custom can generate universal obligation. Obligation is something that *happens to* states in this instance, rather than something they undertake willfully. Hence the tortured formulation "implied consent" to make it appear voluntary.

Customary international law, formulated as "general customary law" is thought of in precisely universal terms; "regional," "special," and "local" custom are the exceptions to the norm.[110] The "persistent objector" rule referred to in Chapter 3, a vestige of pure Voluntarism, still applies, but if a state fails in asserting that it has not become bound because of its persistent objection, this is a likely route for the creation of universal obligation.[111]

Like the mythical universal treaty, this avoids the problems of the Natural Law articulation of universal obligation. Under that conception, obligation was regarded as something either inherent or exogenously imposed, and distinct from human (or state) will (Voluntarism and its cognates, of course, derive from *voluntas,* Latin for "will"). Since the rise to dominance of Voluntarism, universality has been associated with Natural Law thinking, but there is no necessary association between the two. Universal obligations can indeed come about consensually. There is, however, a nonconsensual element even here; states that have not existed from the time when the customary rule *manqué* was still inchoate have not had the opportunity to become persistent objectors. They are born as it were fully encumbered by all existing rules of customary law in force at the time of their statehood.[112]

Positivism also offers no bar to universal obligation. Universality is merely a matter of the *scope* of an obligation; it relates to neither the obligation's character, nor its source or content. Likewise, universality does not necessarily reflect any normative hierarchy among obligations, although it is likely that the norms given the most weight will be those that are universally ascribed to and perhaps vice-versa. Neither Positivism nor Voluntarism conceptually bars obligations having universal scope; obligations may be created to bind all states, and they may evolve from having a narrow scope to universality. This answers one part of the problem. We must now confront the question of whether universal standing to enforce is consistent with the dominant Positivist-Voluntarist normative framework.

If we return to the hypothetical universally subscribed treaty, we have obligation that is *nominally* universal in scope, but is there universal standing to enforce the obligation? As we saw in the previous chapter, one state's violation of its multilateral treaty obligations does not necessarily give any other party standing to make a legal claim in the absence of demonstrated specific injury to the claimant. The dominant normative complex conceptualizes the obligation arising out of multilateral treaties *as if* it were a series of bilateral obligations; it is not generally the case that treaties, even those hypothetically universal in membership give rise to obligations *erga omnes* (except in those cases in which such provision is expressly made or to be inferred from the subject matter). Even in the instance of such multilateral treaties, universal obligation does not translate simply or directly into universal standing.

Two responses immediately arise. As we saw in Chapter 4, Article 48(1)(b) of the *Articles on State Responsibility* does open the door somewhat: "Any State other than an injured State is entitled to invoke the responsibility of another State . . . if; The obligation breached is owed to the international community as a whole." As the Special Rapporteur noted, "The provision intends to give effect to the International Court's statement in the *Barcelona Traction* case" in which it invoked the obligation *erga omnes*. Crawford continues, "Each State is entitled, as a member of the international community as a whole, to invoke the responsibility of another State for breaches of such obligation . . . the obligations in question are by definition collective obligations protecting interests of the international community as such."[113] Although this potentially could allow for straightforward universal jurisdiction because internationally criminalized behavior is regarded as violation of obligations "owed to the community as a whole," a question lingers: what is the legal standing of the *Draft Articles?* Although adopted by the UN General Assembly, they are not a treaty; likewise, although a number of their provisions codify existing customary rules (this is the case with Art 42 cited *supra*), it seems plain that 48(1)(b) is for the time being still in the realm of *lex ferenda*.

A second potential means by which this *aporia* can perhaps be bridged—again in Positivist terms—is by express provision in the treaty for standing without regard to injury. If the ICJ was right in *South west Africa* when the majority stated that the *actio popularis* "is not known to international law as it stands at present," this is one means by which they might become acquainted.[114] With the exception of some human rights treaty regimes (the membership of none of which is universal), this remains in the realm of speculation. Even here, the jurisdictional rules of the various complaint mechanisms tend to be optional rather than compulsory.[115] Even in international human rights law, Voluntarism still seems to dominate.

The absence of many examples, however, is no argument against the approach. If we were to take a broader view of stipulative grants of universal jurisdiction, we would come to the *aut dedere* provision found in a number of treaties. By making it obligatory to prosecute (or extradite), these treaties *eo ipso* grant or acknowledge their parties' right to prosecute (or extradite). One cannot after all, be obliged to do something for which one has no authority.

Grants of jurisdiction such as this provide the opening wedge; although they might never have universal formal membership, these treaties can become binding upon nonmembers through the process of their specific obligations becoming customary law. Here again, we might be blocked by a nonparty state's persistent objection, but even then, as we saw in Chapter 3, this can, in principle, be overridden should the obligation in question be determined to have a peremptory character.

Randall proposes another option, but one about which we must be skeptical. He asserts that ICL treaties with *aut dedere* clauses "may allow nonparties to the conventions to prosecute" violators of those treaties' substantive prohibitions; "all states have the *right* to assume universal jurisdiction over the acts to which the conventions apply."[116] The suggestion is intriguing for the very same reasons it is flawed; it is a direct repudiation of even a vestigial Voluntarism. Although he treats the matter solely in terms of extending powers under a treaty regime to nonparties, as a simple matter of equity—bracketing the provisions of Articles 34–36 of the *Vienna Convention*—if a state is to gain benefits from a treaty to which it is not party, it must reciprocally undertake the obligations of that treaty. If third states are going to be able to enforce the rules of the treaty against parties, they should, as a matter of both logic and equity, be held subject to those same rules. Randall is in fact proposing to make states directly subject to treaties to which they have chosen not to become parties; he is arguing in Positivist terms for Natural Law-like wholly exogenous imposition of obligation. Bruce Broomhall is correct in his reminder that in treaties "setting out a regime of 'universal jurisdiction' . . . this form of jurisdiction is not truly 'universal' but is a regime of jurisdictional rights and obligations arising among a closed set of states' parties."[117] Randall's wishful thinking aside, nothing short of achieving customary law status will bind third parties to the rules contained in a treaty.

It is by now clear, that universal obligation and universal jurisdiction to enforce such obligations can come about through the simplest of Positivist-Voluntarist means. Although universal jurisdiction to enforce an earlier version of international society's fundamental norms was rooted in Natural Law—as were the fundamental norms—there is nothing intrinsically Naturalist to the idea of universal jurisdiction. While this does represent a manifestation of the old practice, like its cognates surveyed in the preceding two chapters, it represents a return conditioned by the current normative climate that is at the same time establishing a new climate. Universal jurisdiction comes closer to capturing the ethos and dynamics of classical international punishment than anything yet surveyed, even third party countermeasures in response to violations of obligations *erga omnes*. The fundamental (and obvious) difference between universal jurisdiction and classical international punishment is that the sole subjects of universal jurisdiction are individuals. In the next chapter, we will analyze what amount to attempts to bring back the old practice in its totality.

CHAPTER 6

The Problematic Discourse
of State Crime

We come finally to contemporary efforts to bring back the classical practice of international punishment in its nearly complete form; as we will see, the only significant way in which what is advocated today differs from the old practice is in the lack of reliance on Natural Law metaphysics. Contemporary discussion of the criminalization of state behavior and the punishment of states for the commission of international crimes effectively brings us full circle to Grotius and Locke.

The Conceptual Problem

One of the insights Constructivism has brought IR is that our world is, in part, made what it is by what we *say* about it. To an extent, we make things what they are by saying what they are.[1] One way by which we do this is the use of metaphor; by asserting that one thing is another thing. We can see this issue at play in debates over the ontological status and personality of the state.[2] Does saying that a state is a person *make* it a person?

Of particular relevance for the issue of international punishment is the question: can states *per se* commit crimes? Are states subject to punishment?[3] Deceptively simple arguments have been given both in favor of and in opposition to the proposition of state criminality. Neither position offers an argument that is sufficient or compelling. By analyzing state criminality in terms of state personality and vice versa, and by analyzing the conceptual history of the idea of the state as person, and examining the conceptual and rhetorical underpinnings of the idea of state personality, the debate about the personality of the state will take a very different direction. Conversely, by looking at the question of state personality through the lens of some of its logical implications, new concerns arise. While it is possible and perfectly tenable to remain agnostic about the ontological status of states, it is untenable to treat their *legal and moral* personality as anything other than metaphorical or "as-if"; they therefore can neither commit crimes nor incur punishment.

Preliminary Arguments for State Crime as a Conceptual and Legal Category

In support of the idea of state criminality lies the traditional analogy—going back at least to Grotius and Hobbes, but with clear antecedents in the ancient world—between the state and the individual, and the language of the state as person; these tropes are conceptual fundaments of both IR and International Law. At some level, we recognize them as heuristic simplifications, such as when we speak of states acting and having interests. In asserting something to be a state interest, or asserting that some action has been taken by a state, empirically, the state stands in for the aggregation of individuals comprising this merely notional entity.[4]

An appropriation of Hobbes's wonderful metaphor, the famous composite, artificial person from the frontispiece from *Leviathan* is apposite here. In Hobbes's image the state is a person who has passions, who wills, reasons, acts and has rights that derive from but are independent of and go beyond those of the citizens. This understanding was reconfigured by Pufendorf, who added to the metaphor the idea of states being simultaneously rights bearers and duty bearers—duties that went beyond being simple corollaries of the rights of individuals.[5] With Hegel, the metaphor of the state as a person became fully hypostatized.[6] It is now deeply internalized, and while it is subject to scholarly questioning, it still forms the commonsense of the discipline, the policy community and public discourse.

The situation is very similar in international law, which *treats* the state as an actor that carries rights, duties and responsibilities. Obligations undertaken on behalf of the state by the agents of one government survive changes of government because the obligation is conceptualized as attaching to the state, albeit for the expressly practical reason of maintaining the continuity of obligations, rather than from any metaphysical commitments. Conversely, when a state is held responsible for a wrongful act and compensation is ordered, the liability will survive the replacement of the malfeasant government. It is acknowledged that materially individuals are the actors, and that they create obligations for their states, but through the Act of State Doctrine, their acts are *considered* the acts of their state; their acts are *imputed* to the state (assuming certain criteria are satisfied).[7] Traditionally, this has also had the effect of shielding state agents from any legal responsibility (tortious or criminal) for their acts on behalf of the state.

In this regime—built upon the same hypostatized metaphor—the argument in favor of considering certain state behaviors criminal and attaching penal liability to them is that if states act, if they have rights (stipulatively), duties (stipulatively), and responsibilities (stipulatively), then the violation of certain of their responsibilities might rise to the level of criminality. We must analyze whether this trope can support the weight of this attribution.

A more strictly Positivist argument for the acceptance of the state crime as a legal category has been offered by Nina Jørgensen, who has suggested two possibilities. Because corporate crime and criminality are accepted so widely, they may qualify as general principles of law, and by analogy, the state as a corporate actor can likewise be held criminally liable for any acts stipulated to be unlawful. Alternately, she suggests that state practice indicates the acceptance of state criminal responsibility and is thus indicative of "an emerging category of customary international law."[8] The second of these suggestions must be evaluated empirically, but certainly the decision *not* to adopt the category on the occasions it has been discussed must count as damning evidence against her assertion of a customary basis. Her first suggestion, resting on an analogy with corporations, is more promising, and relates in many ways to the general argument introduced previously; however, the following sections will undermine the strength of the analogy.

Preliminary Arguments against State Crime as a Conceptual and Legal Category

The common argument against the viability of the category of crimes of states rests less on trope and legal fiction and more on a reductive legal Positivism. Current international law as it exists simply does not countenance the concept of state crime, and when the issue has come up, the adoption of rules criminalizing certain state behaviors as such has been explicitly rejected. In both the Rome Statute (Art. 25) and the Articles on the Responsibility of States for Internationally Wrongful Acts (Art. 40), international law and the International Law Commission in particular have unambiguously held that only individuals (even acting collectively) commit international crimes.[9] *Stricto sensu,* black letter allows only that states can commit delicts or "serious breaches" of international law. Because both crimes and delicts give rise to liability (and, in principle, sanction), the difference may seem simply to be semantic, but that appearance is challenged by the resistance and dissatisfaction of scholars who insist on the need for a legal category that encompasses crimes committed by states.

Earlier drafts of the Articles on State Responsibility did include provision for state crimes:

Article 19

International Crimes and Delicts

1. An act of a State which constitutes a breach of an international obligation is an internationally wrongful act, regardless of the subject-matter of the obligation breached.

2. An internationally wrongful act which results from the breach by a State of an international obligation so essential for the protection of fundamental interests of the international community that its breach is recognized as

a crime by that community as a whole constitutes an international crime.

The exclusion of Article 19 (and the related Articles 40(3) and 51–53 addressing scope and sanction, respectively) from the Draft Articles and the unwillingness to countenance the inclusion of such an article in the Rome Statute ends the matter for many.[10]

Matters are more complicated than this, however. Georges Abi-Saab reminds us that the purpose of Article 19 was never about creating a penal law; instead, the aim was to create another tier of responsibility, albeit one that used the language of 'crime' based on the gravity of the violated obligation.[11] Alain Pellet insists, however, the type of responsibility invoked in the Draft Articles, the use of the term "crime" notwithstanding, was "neither civil nor penal, it was simply 'international.'"[12] This type of responsibility would depart from the normal model of strictly bilateral responsibility to a model of responsibility *erga omnes*. Under this type of obligation, "*all other states*" were counted for legal purposes as injured, and Article 40 (3), in fact, made specific reference to the idea of the obligation *erga omnes*.[13] Despite these assurances, James Crawford asserts that the reluctance to accept the idea of international crimes of state derived from the reluctance, even among supporters of the idea "to accept a full-scale penal regime, or indeed any punitive elements at all."[14]

In one respect, these are critiques are surely correct: *nulla poena sine crimen,* but they also miss a larger point, and are still beholden to the Hobbesian trope. It is my contention that both sides in the debate, but especially the advocates of state crime and punishment, rest their positions upon faulty premises, at the core of which are a misunderstanding of intention and an improper analogy to other notions of corporate criminality found in domestic legal systems.

The Corporeal Metaphor I: Antecedents to the State as Person

The attribution of "legal" personality is a metaphor by which nonhuman, nonconscious entities (usually collectives) are described in the discourse of law to have mental and moral consciousness.[15]

Because so much turns on the question of the legal personality of states, it is worth investigating the development of this trope. Although our metaphor of the state as person derives from Hobbes, the trope of speaking of nonhumans or groups of humans collectively as persons (or originally "bodies") has a much deeper genealogy. The very word "corporation" already reveals the metaphorical roots of what we are discussing.

Corpora *in Roman Law*

Debates very similar to those regarding the personality of the state have swirled around the corporation for some time. Roman law is our source for the very concept of a corporation, and many debates stem from the way in which the Romans articulated the agency, rights and status of corporations. For them, to speak of a group of persons collectively holding rights was explicitly a *fiction* of the law, something not literally true, but treated *as if* it were true for certain specific purposes.[16] "Roman lawyers were quite aware that some bodies, groups, were recognized by law as able to own and sue, and in that respect as different from other bodies."[17] Groups of individual persons were regarded for legal purposes as having rights and duties collectively, and although they were *treated* as if they were persons under the law, they were not *described* as persons. Peter French, however, holds that anything that was allowed to be a party to a legal dispute was referred to as a person, but offers no textual support. Measured against the abundance of textual support P.W. Duff provides, French's assertion cannot hold. [18] The Romans' preferred terminology was *corpus,* a body: "A *persona* is *singularis,* a *corpus* complex and composed of several *personae* acting as a unit...whatever they do, ten men will never make one *persona*...Any set of men who are for any purpose regarded as a group may be called a *corpus.*"[19] This distinction will be of central importance below because the language of bodies conveys no necessary connotation of mind, while the language of person and personality does.

Alongside *corpus,* we sometimes find *universitas* (D.3.4.7.1) a term that signified "a whole as contrasted with its parts, or . . . a group as contrasted with its members." Particular manifestations of *corpora* or *universitates* included *societates, collegia,* churches, *municipia* (D.48.18.1.7) and the state itself: "Sometimes . . . *corpora* stretches so as to cover the bodies of men politically organized, towns, the State, the Senate, the plebs. All are bodies."[20] Although there was some variation between categories, the members of a *corpus* were generally able to collectively own property (including slaves), inherit, and were granted standing under the law to be represented in their own right before the courts—all things that persons can do.[21] It is important to note, however, that Roman law was inconsistent across time and category about whether it was the fictional body, or its constituent natural persons that held these rights and obligations.[22]

The corpus *of the Church and the Body of Christ*

The grant to churches of *corpus* in Roman law complements an analogous move in the early history of Christianity in which the Church (both the institution and the congregation—Church as *universitas*) was equated doctrinally with the Body of Christ ("The Church was One and Indivisible, the Body of Christ"). In legal rather than theological terms, this meant, "ownership of all Church property was [attributed] either to God Himself . . . or the His Body the Church."[23]

Corporeal language is a central part of Christian theology; *Colossians* 1:18 states that "The Head of the Body is Christ . . . He is the head of the Body which is the Church."[24] These are articulations of positions established early in the Church's history, contemporaneous and clearly indebted to the Roman concept of corporation.

The equation of the church with the body of Christ is traceable—in addition to the reference to Colossians made earlier—to statements by Paul in I *Corinthians, Ephesians* and *Romans,* but the particular term, "mystical body" of Christ, originally had a different connotation. The "mystical body" was not at first the notion of the church as *universitas,* but instead referred to the transubstantiated "consecrated host." It was the influence of the rediscovery of Roman law and the importation of its ideas into Canon law in the twelfth century that led to the transformation of the terminology; " 'mystical body,' which originally had a liturgical or sacramental meaning, took on a connotation of sociological content."[25] The identification of the church with the body of Christ was affirmed by the Bull *Unam Sanctum* in 1302 in which Boniface VIII stated that the church "represents one mystical body, the head of which is Christ, and the head of Christ is God."[26]

It was to bolster this appropriation of religious terminology, that the doctrine of Christ's two bodies was developed: the true body in the form of the transubstantiated host, and the mystical body in the form of the Church. Kantorowicz quotes Simon of Tournai on this: "Two are the bodies of Christ: the human material body which he assumed from the Virgin, and the spiritual collegiate body, the ecclesiastical college." The debt to Roman legal thought could hardly be clearer.

Giving content to the mystical body extended this trope; Isaac of Stella disaggregated the body by including not only Christ as the head, but the priesthood as the limbs.[27] The flock became "members," in Latin *membra* (limbs, body parts, organs). The trope was given definitive redirection by Aquinas, who changed the language from the mystical body of *Christ,* to the mystical body of *the Church.*

> Now . . . the Church, which had been *the* mystical body of Christ, became *a* mystical body in its own right . . . the Church organism became a "mystical body" in an almost juristic sense: a mystical corporation . . . The *Corpus Christi* had been changed into a corporation of Christ.[28]

In all of this, however, the Church was never understood to be a *person;* it remained always a *body.* With this background, in the next section I turn to the more specific question of how the language of corporeality has influenced discussion of the state as an intentional actor.

The Corporeal Metaphor II: The Origins of State Personality

> Crimes against international law are committed by men, not by abstract entities, and only by punishing individuals who commit such crimes can the provisions of international law be enforced.[29]

> Although they seem real enough to their citizens, States are juridical abstractions.[30]

Thomas Hobbes and the Person of the State

Thomas Hobbes's conceptions of representation and "personation" are central developments in this story, because they represent the transformation of the idea of a collective body to the state. While the Romans did use the language of the *corpus* of the state, and Hobbes builds upon the Roman formulation, it is his adaptation and Pufendorf's emendations of it that are really responsible for the notion of the state as actor, which is fundamental to IR, and is presupposed by advocates and critics of the idea of state criminality.

Hobbes, of course, was not the first to utilize this language; we have already seen the Roman use of *corpus* in reference to the state, and the equation (or at least equivalence) of the state with the human body predates Rome. We find it also in *The Politics* (1253a) but at this stage, it is mere analogy, not even metaphor. Outside of the Roman *corpus juris civilis,* Cicero utilized this imagery in *De Officis* (III.22), and Seneca in *De Ira* (II.31) and *De Clementia* (I.5.1).[31]

In the medieval period, these tropes—still closely linked to the Church's utilization of corporeal language—were put to aims similar to those of the Church. Kantorowicz invokes Baldus's rendering of the *populus* as a "mystical body": "A *populus* was not simply the sum of individuals of a community, but 'men assembled into one mystical body' (*hominum collectio in unum corpus mysticum*), men forming . . . a body or corporation to be grasped only intellectually, since it was not a real or material body."[32] To emphasize, however, they asserted the *corporeality* of the group, never its *person*ality. There were a number of variations upon this theme of the corporeality of the state; one common variation was the state's marriage to the ruler.[33] Others, borrowing from Seneca, identified the ruler with the soul and the state with the body. The most common characterization, however, mirrored in secularized fashion that used by the Church: the Prince was the head of a body itself composed of the people.[34] In this body, every part had its "particular place and task . . . Although every member constituted a vital part of the . . . whole . . . this whole was not affected by the changes of its many parts."[35]

In England, there was a lengthy tradition of corporealizing the state of which Hobbes was inheritor and systematizer. Only a few decades before Hobbes published *Leviathan,* James I combined a number of the tropes we have seen so far, announcing to Parliament: " 'What God hath conjoined then, let no man separate.' I am the husband, and all the whole island is my lawful wife; I am the head, and it is my body." Prior to Hobbes, however, the best-known English usage of the corporeal metaphor was that of John of Salisbury in *Policraticus.* The trope was also picked up in France by Jean Bodin, for whom the state had both a body and a soul. Throughout this arc, however, the significance of these tropes remained to be worked out in any detail, and it is for this reason that Hobbes's contribution is central.

Hannah Pitkin and Quentin Skinner have extensively detailed the evolution of Hobbes's idea of the state as a "purely artificial" person.[36] The core of Hobbes's position is that when all of the people, the "multitude," jointly contract to submit their wills to a chosen representative, that representative *becomes* an artificial person; it carries their personality or "personates" them.[37] "The only means, according to Hobbes, by which a multitude can manage to 'institute' a commonwealth is by transforming themselves into an 'artificial person' by way of authorizing some natural person or persons to represent them."[38] The chosen representative, the artificial person who represents all of the natural persons and wields the combined power of the populace, is, of course, the sovereign, the bearer of the "Person of the State."[39] This act of contracting *creates* the body politic, what Hobbes also calls the "civil person" or the state. By eliding person and body, artificial/civil *person* and *body* politic, Hobbes changed the metaphor, and created the (pleonastic) corporate *person,* opening the door to a new set of associations—especially cognitive—that body does not entail.

For Hobbes, artificial persons are often also natural persons.[40] In Hobbes, artificial personality is a *role* or *office* rather than an ontological signification. Persons act; they may be distinguished in terms of the origins of their actions. Some persons' acts are their own; they are natural persons—another variance from familiar usage where "natural" connotes biological. Some persons' acts represent others; Hobbes calls them feigned or artificial persons.[41] Acting in the manner of a representative of another—acting *as* them or *for* them—is to bear their person. One individual can bear one other individual's person, or one individual can bear the persons of many—hence the sovereign makes the multitude into a single person by being their sole representative. The unity of the representative is what makes the person one. It is what makes the multitude into a single civil person.[42]

When one person acts on behalf of another, the former is the actor, and the latter is the author—the author of the representative's actions. Acting on behalf of the author is to act with authority.[43] Because the people have authorized the artificial person, the sovereign, to act on their behalf, they are the *authors* of the sovereign's acts and bear responsibility for them regardless of whether the "author" ordered, consented to, or willed those acts. Hobbes indicates that the people are to be understood as having willed whatever act the sovereign takes.[44] It is *as if* they willed the acts of the sovereign. Therefore, they likewise undertake responsibility for any pledges the sovereign makes as their representative.[45]

In this rendering (and the political configuration it represented), there is a relationship of identity between the state and its ruler. In his capacity as the representative of all the people, the head of state is an artificial person; he also *is* the state. "The rulers *are* the state; their interests the state interests; their will the state's will."[46] Looked at from the other way round, the state is a person because it possesses a single will; wherever there is one will for all, there is one person. The state therefore is one person, and its will is also the citizenry's will.[47]

> A Multitude of men, are made *One* Person, when they are by one man, or one Person, Represented; so that it be done with the consent of every one of that Multitude in particular. For it is the *Unity* of the Representer, not the *Unity* of the Represented, that maketh the Person *One*. And it is the Representer that beareth the Person, and but one Person . . . [48]

> This is more than Consent, or Concord; it is a reall Unitie of them all, in one and the same Person. [49]

In *De Cive,* Hobbes makes the ruler the soul of the body/person; "Because man has a soul, he has a will, that is he can assent and refuse; similarly a commonwealth has a will, and can assent and refuse through the holder of sovereign power, and only so."[50] This formulation changes in *Leviathan* to the Introduction's famous anatomy of the artificial person. Here the soul is no longer the sovereign *per se* but sovereignty; sovereignty is the artificial soul that gives "life and motion to the whole body."

Hobbes's account bears some similarities—especially in language—to the accounts we saw previously; Hobbes's particular usages differ from them in some important ways, but they share a number of fundaments. In all of these cases, we find either bodies or artificial persons aggregated from individuals, and—at least with Hobbes—acting with discrete wills and able to contract.

It is not clear, however, that Hobbes would be willing to countenance the possibility that the "purely artificial person of the state" could commit crimes, or that the populace as a whole would be necessarily liable if the state were to commit a crime. Again, the issue rests on authorization and representation; although the multitude is understood to be that author of the sovereign's acts, a natural person, an author, can only grant to their representative the authority to do that which they possess the right to undertake. As a matter of logical semantics, we do not possess the right to commit crimes (we cannot possess the right to do what we are forbidden or to forego what we are obliged), so we cannot transmit that right to a representative. It is likewise a truism for Hobbes that if a representative were to do something that the author could not authorize, not personally possessing that right, it cannot be attributed to the author.

It cannot therefore, be attributed to the artificial person. As Hobbes says in the context of Covenants made by artificial persons,

> . . . when the Actor maketh a Covenant by Authority, he bindeth thereby the Author, no lesse than if he had made it himself; and no lesse subjecteth him to all the consequences of the same. And therefore all that hath been said formerly . . . of the nature of Covenants between man and man in their naturall capacity, is true also when they are made by their Actors, Representers, or Procurators that have authority from them, so far-forth as is in their Commission, *but no farther . . . For no man is obliged by a Covenant, whereof he is not Author; nor consequently by a Covenant made against, or beside the Authority he gave . . . so when the Authority is feigned, it obligeth the Actor onely; there being no author but himselfe.*[51]

What Hobbes says specifically about promising applies *a fortiori* to all acts from which derive either obligation or liability. If the actor acts with authority, their acts will bind (or impute liability to) their author; in the absence of authority, either express or derivative, no obligation or liability will be transferred—the actor is in that instance the author as well, the represented natural person is not. He does not allow, however, that the people might make this determination, but this does not bear upon the *external* evaluation of acts ascribed to the state.

There is, of course, a more direct reason that Hobbes would not countenance the possibility of state crime; going back to his particular conception of the State of Nature in *Leviathan* I.XIII, there is no possibility of crime, because there neither is nor can be law; for Hobbes, without law, there definitionally can be no crime. Like Grotius, Hobbes held that states could only do those things that individuals could do in their original condition; in Hobbes's State of Nature (but not Grotius's), there were no moral restrictions on what an individual might do because there was neither law nor right nor wrong. More precisely, Hobbes allowed that natural humans *might* learn moral obligations to others, but these would only bind *in foro interno,* but were not externally binding and were therefore unenforceable; in the Latin version of *Leviathan* Hobbes explicitly indicates that violations of these obligations are not crimes.[52] There is nothing in *Leviathan* I.XIII.12 to indicate that he felt that this was in any regard different in the State of Nature within which states were posited to exist. Thus, it was for Hobbes a conceptual impossibility for states to commit crimes. Advocates of state criminality might turn instead to Pufendorf for support; he did assert that there are binding obligations in the State of Nature, and carries that association forward into the international State of Nature, but he explicitly rejects the idea of international punishment, and it is unclear that his mode of Natural Law reasoning would be congenial to punishment advocates.[53] We find ourselves in a situation in which the very conceptual underpinnings of the idea of crimes of states are undermined at the very origin of the language of state personality—Hobbes is no friend to those who would make the artificial person an international criminal body.[54]

The Corporeal Metaphor III: Corporations, Corporate Crime, and Corporate Punishment

Corporate Personality

> [W]hen a jurist first said 'A corporation is a person,' he was using a *metaphor* to express the truth that a corporation bears some analogy or resemblance to a person, and is to be treated in law in certain respects *as if* it were a person, or a rational being capable of feeling and volition.[55]

> The misinterpretation of the anthropomorphic metaphor 'juristic person' as a real entity . . . is the unpermissible hypostatization of a thinking aid or auxiliary concept constructed by jurisprudence merely for the purpose of simplifying and illustrating the description of a complex legal situation.[56]

Hobbes utilized a somewhat different notion of artificial person from what is found in discussions of the personality of the corporation and elsewhere. Hobbes felt that a natural person could simultaneously be an artificial person if they represent others; modern law, while utilizing Hobbes's pleonasm of "corporate person," holds closer to older usages in treating the corporate person as something separate from all of the natural persons that make it up. While the law treats corporations as persons, the nature of this legal personality has long been disputed.[57] The Fiction Theory, exemplified in the work of Friedrich Carl von Savigny and Rudolf von Ihering, held that "the personality...of the corporation is not natural—it is fictitious."[58] For Savigny, "corporate property belonged to a fictitious being and not to any real person or entity...ownership involves the possession of a will by the owner; and...inasmuch as a corporation does not really possess a will, it must as a property-owner be a fictitious person."[59]

Von Iherring agreed that the legal personality of the corporation is a fiction, or indeed a metaphor, but insisted that this was also the case with the very *existence* of the corporation. "[T]he fictitious personality is not 'created' by the state, because it does not exist.... a corporation is merely an abbreviated way of writing the names of the several members."[60] Therefore, the putative rights of the corporation are, in fact, the rights of the members, not of some notional entity.[61]

Elaborating on the idea of corporate personality as metaphor, Morris Cohen asserted that "to speak...of the union or group as having a single mind is a convenient but dangerous metaphor...this use of the language of identity for two different things that are in some way analogous is precisely what constitutes the nature of fiction."[62] "The corporation is given personality" and that whatever will the law understands it to have is a "delegated will...the corporation is invisible and *in abstracto*. It has no human wants."[63] It likewise does not act per se: "When we speak of an act or an attribute as corporate, it is not corporate in the psychologically collective sense, but merely representative, and imputed to the corporation for reason of policy and convenience."[64] Harold Laski cites Chief Justice Marshall on this point: "[The corporation] is...an artificial being, invisible, intangible, and *existing only in contemplation of law*."[65]

Opposed to these skeptical, nominalist understandings of the personality of corporations is the Realist or Person Theory most closely associated with Otto Gierke, for whom the personality of the corporation "is neither fictitious, nor artificial, nor created by the state, but both real and natural, recognized but not created by the law...When a corporation is formed by the union of natural persons, *a new real person, a real corporate 'organism', is brought into being.*"[66] Most important, for those subscribing to this view, the corporation, as a real entity, exists independent of the individual, natural persons making it up.[67] Other figures in this tradition carried the corporeality metaphor further, endowing the corporation with organs, gender, will and senses. The third of these attributions, in particular, has become the central point of contention.[68]

Corporate Liability

When turning to the question of corporate criminal liability and punishment, courts tended to find that corporations could not be prosecuted for "crimes requiring intent," because lacking minds, they could not possess a "corrupted mind."[69] As Laski summarized the matter, crimes requiring intent require a mind, but the corporation "cannot have a mind at all." He believed, however, that the law might need to *attribute* a mind to corporation so that it might *infer* intent, a mental state, to acts attributable to the corporation.[70] The way around this has generally been to *impute* the intent of the agents or representatives of the corporation to the corporation itself. " . . . the corporation is liable for the acts and intents of its employees, acting on behalf of the corporation, which are imputed to the entity."[71]

In this approach, an outgrowth of the rule *respondeat superior,* "corporate responsibility is always derivative. It must always be located through the responsibility of an individual actor. An individual first commits the offense; the responsibility of that individual is then imputed to the corporation . . . if there is no individual responsibility, there can be no corporate responsibility."[72] The stipulation that the initial wrongful act must always be made by a flesh-and-blood natural person is central. "Speaking of corporate conduct or corporate fault is . . . a shorthand way of referring to the conduct and culpability of the individual members of the collectivity.."[73] Utilizing the corporeal metaphor to its fullest (if perhaps rather un-self-consciously), Lord Justice Denning further explicated the imputational approach in *Bolton v. Graham & Sons* (1956):

> A company may in many ways be likened to a human body. It has a brain and nerve centre which control what it does. It also has hands which hold the tools and act in accordance with directions from the centre. Some of the *people* in the company are mere servants and agents who are nothing more than hands to do the work and cannot be said to represent the mind or will. Others are directors and managers who *represent* the directing mind and will of the company, and control what it does. *The state of mind of these managers is the state of mind of the company.*[74]

The most nuanced version of the imputational approach, and the one that comes closest to the Realists, is Larry May's; he retains the view that responsibility for acts must be imputed to the corporation from the conduct of its employees because "corporations can only act vicariously."[75] Despite individuals always being the material actors, their place within the corporation, their acting from corporate directives links their acts to the corporation. "The best way to conceive of corporate actions is on the model of vicarious agency . . . corporate actions are really only very complex arrangements of joint and vicarious actions of individual persons."[76] He then qualifies this view by insisting that the agent's act must be in furtherance of a decision made by an appropriately authorized senior manager.

Matters, however, are simpler for corporate Realists, for whom the corporation, as a real person, has a mind and thus may form intent, and may therefore possess the *mens rea* necessary for subjective criminal liability. "When a corporation is guilty of crime it is because of a corporate act, a corporate intent . . . The fact that a corporation can act only by human agents is immaterial."[77] *Inter alia,* Ann Foerschler, Peter French, Celia Wells, William S. Laufer and C.M.V. Clarkson have suggested ways to articulate what they consider a meaningful Realist notion of corporate intent, insistent that the corporation *must* be treated as capable of forming intents *suo iure:* "Corporations exhibit their own special kind of intentionality, namely corporate policy."[78]

French, upon whose account Alexander Wendt largely bases his own and Toni Erskine hers, is primarily concerned with the *moral* personality of corporations.[79] The lynchpin of his account is the attribution of intentionality to the corporation's "Internal Decision Structure," a move that he feels "licenses the predication of corporate intentionality."[80] The CIDS works to aggregate the decisions, intentions and acts of individual natural persons within the corporation into a "corporate decision"; it "*incorporates* acts of biological persons."[81] For French, any decision taken in accordance with a CIDS is to be understood, not at all figuratively, as the *corporation's* decision. For French, corporations make decisions; antecedent to decision, he attributes interests and reasons to them; as a result, they therefore also have intentions and take actions. This is emphatically not a metaphor for French; talk of corporations having reasons and intents, acting and consequently bearing responsibility is quite literal. Foerschler follows French's account quite closely, but also makes the *structure* of the corporation a causal actor.[82]

As the realists approach the matter, it is necessary to look not only at the natural persons composing a corporation, but also at their *relationships*. The corporation affects the conduct of individuals; as an institution it can "possess knowledge or means of knowledge that may be unavailable in total to any single individual."[83] They turn us away from the notion of intention as a subjective, individual mental state, and toward an understanding that is almost wholly inferential. "[R]eference to the policies pursued by a corporation may be a reference to the rationale that makes sense of its actions rather than to any goals that have been identified and articulated by the participants.... intent can be attributed to a set of policies... *The intent is the rationale that presents the best explanation of the corporation's policies.*"[84] Laufer goes furthest in explicating an account of "corporate mental states."[85]

By following this path, however, it potentially becomes necessary for the Realists to infer not just intent, but also the existence and content of the very policy from which the intent is to be inferred when there is no actual statement of policy. Again, the inference is based upon the deduction of the "most reasonable explanation of the conduct of that corporation"— a standard that is more subjective than they might like to admit.[86] This is a delicate tissue indeed when the underlying motivation is the attribution of criminal responsibility and the levying of punishment.

Corporate Punishment

The attribution of conduct and criminal intent to corporations and the imposition upon them of criminal liability is ethically troubling for some, and the parallels with the punishment of states are obvious. Cohen was insistent that in attributing intent to a collection of individuals "we are apt to forget 'its' action may simply be the action of certain individuals in authority."[87] However, if corporations are subjected to punishment for violating the laws to which the state subjects them, "punishment . . . may be inflicted upon the corporate entity, but in so doing, the law is using the corporate entity as a mere means of reaching the human beings who act for the corporation."[88]

The problem with even this understanding is that the punishment does not *only* reach the "human beings who act for the corporation"; indeed, the effects are significantly broader:

> [C]onsideration must . . . be given to the 'spillover' effect of corporate sanctions onto persons, such as shareholders, who are removed from the commission of the offense. The standard dismissal of the significance of spillover effects is that those who reap the benefits of corporate wrongdoing must be prepared to incur the costs. Yet . . . those who will be affected . . . cannot adequately protect themselves against this risk . . . *The spillover effects are indiscriminate.*[89]

As Max Radin makes clear, a putative corporate punishment is, in actuality *designed* to harm individuals in no way linked to the formulation of the criminal policy or its execution, and again, it does so indiscriminately. "[The] apparent punishment of the corporation as such will not stand analysis. It is obvious that when the corporation's property is taken, the shareholders must be the sufferers. *If they did not suffer in any way, there would be no point in punishing the corporation.*"[90]

Not all commentators are concerned; French and Clarkson, in particular, are unsympathetic to the fates of innocent employees or shareholders, the latter in particular for having voluntarily assumed the risks associated with investing.[91] However, they miss a fundamental distinction between commercial risk, which investors can be held knowingly and voluntarily to undertake, and noncommercial risk, which no account can reasonably postulate they undertake. It is simply untenable to assert that investors can be held to have voluntarily undertaken the risk that those acting as agents of the company in which they have invested might act illegally and face sanction that would harm the interests of the investors. To assert otherwise is, in fact to assert the investors' willing and knowing participation in a criminal conspiracy merely by having invested in a corporation.

Evaluating the Prospects of State Criminality

We have seen a number of tropes in play so far. In Roman law, a group could constitute a body for legal purposes; in Christian Theology, a group could likewise constitute a *mystical* body. In Medieval political thought, the *populus* could constitute a mystical body. It was only with Hobbes that the equation and its signification changed. Despite carefully detailing the etymology of "person," Hobbes is remarkably lax in sliding back and forth between person and body, using body politic and person interchangeably, even in his Latin writings. From Hobbes, through twentieth-century corporate law, down to IR current advocates of state personality and state crime, the group is now regarded as constituting a person *simpliciter* with all that personality entails. Much hinges on this change; persons—unlike bodies—can reason, form intentions, and bear obligations. When speaking of bodies, there is no necessary connotation of mind. Blindly following Hobbes, we have slid very carelessly from the fiction that a group is a body (*corpus*), to the assertion that a body is a person. More completely parsed, the position underpinning advocacy of state criminality is that group = body = person. Although remembering that this was a move the Roman initiators of this metaphor explicitly rejected does not settle matters, it does raise the question of why they rejected regarding groups as persons.

To finally evaluate the tenability of asserting the personality of states for purposes of international criminal liability, we need to look closely at our understandings of a number of concepts in addition to the state as actor: crime (responsibility and liability) and antecedent to the latter, intention. There are also political and ethical questions related to the *consequences* of adopting the idea of state criminality: if the state can commit, and thus be held responsible for, crimes, *who* is to be punished? If the state is punished collectively—and if we *provisionally* accept that it is a composite or artificial person, this is the only way in which it can be punished—how is the resulting punishment of parties (citizens) who had no part in the design or execution of the unlawful act to be justified?[92] There are obvious parallels with the moral questions surrounding international sanctions because the modes of punishment tend in most accounts to follow the model of international sanctions, although strictly speaking, international sanctions are punitive without being penal.

With regard to the question of states acting, the real question is how far we want to take as literal something that has been from its outset avowedly *metaphoric* and *fictive*. If we want to attach criminal liability to the state for violating certain types of obligation, we need to be very certain about the tenability of this trope and how far we might extend it. Like corporations, the attribution of rights and duties to states is a fiction, the remnant of a trope we forgot was a trope; as a result, to claim that states can commit crimes, they must be able to form (beyond mere imputation or fiction) the requisite intention and *mens rea*. We must be able to attribute intention and *mens rea* to states in more than a rhetorical or figurative sense. The trope of the state as person, however, simply cannot support the weight of this demand. In domestic legal contexts, as we have seen, it is held to be the case (but not unproblematically so) that legal persons other than individuals can act intentionally and may thus be subject to criminal sanction for violating the law, but it is premature to leap from this norm to treating the state in the same way *simpliciter*.

Articulating (State) Intention

Accounts of state crime and state punishment uniformly work from a direct analogy between the state and the corporation as an intentional actor. In order to determine the aptness of treating states as intentional actors subject to liability and punishment, it is essential to work out what it means to act intentionally. In order to determine if states can commit crimes, besides examining the meaningfulness of attribution to them of actions, we need to ascertain if there is any meaningful sense in which we might say that they intend.

Following Donald Davidson, we might say that at its most basic, to act intentionally is to act from (or in accordance with) a statable *reason* itself based upon certain statable *beliefs* in pursuit of articulable *desires*.[93] To assert that states act intentionally it must be possible to attribute to them an entire complex of mental states. There are long traditions of speaking of states as having interests, and of states' reason *(raison d'etat)*, but except in cases of the blindest adherence to the Hobbesian metaphor, or the most tortuous of metaphysical contortions, these are— and have always been—no more than rhetorical devices. To speak of state intentions, we need to countenance the existence of not only state reasons, but also state beliefs and state desires.

In the Hobbesian tradition, the state is a person, and not just a body. As a person rather than merely a body, it is possesses a mind, reason and all that is associated with reason. Hobbes's transformation is essential. If we restrict ourselves to Hobbesian imagery this attribution is perhaps no great leap; indeed when we bear in mind the political configurations Hobbes's writings described (reflected and advocated), it is not difficult to speak of *that* sort of state having interests and beliefs, forming intentions and acting because the state was its sovereign and vice versa. The mental states of the state were the sovereign's mental states.

The language of "reason of state" is actually older than Hobbes's appropriation of corporeal imagery, but came very easily to complement it.[94] There are cognate concepts to be found in Cicero and Tacitus, but the formulation with which we are most familiar has fifteenth- and sixteenth-century origins.[95] Throughout its conceptual development, this phrase connoted merely the idea that a human agent acting on behalf of a state was allowed to engage in conduct not normally allowed a private citizen in a nonpolitical context. States were not held to have reason or reasons *per se;* the justification or legitimization of certain normally impermissible acts was found in the *reason* for which they were committed. *The reason was the state,* but no one was attributing a mind or mental states to the state. It was only with the subsumption of this trope to the imagery of Hobbes, however, that it came from the late seventeenth century to have cognitive associations while retaining its original political meaning. From this point, the *state* was considered able to act in ways and do things that were impermissible to other persons—natural or legal—in other contexts. It was only by accepting this trope built upon an antecedent trope that the language of states forming and possessing intentions became intelligible. As a basis for the attribution or imputation of intents, however, it is insufficient.

State Personality in IR Theory and International Legal Theory

The issue is not simply that we are burdened by un-reflected-upon inheritances from early modern thought; Alexander Wendt is very concerned to identify the state as a person, indeed as an intentional actor and perhaps an organism or "superorganism."[96] In his account, he goes to great pains to justify the tenability of the state as the most important actor in IR, ultimately by treating it in Scientific Realist terms as an unobservable. Wendt insists that states are *real things,* out there, acting intentionally but unobservable, and that IR cannot do without them conceptually. Without positing their personality, we allegedly cannot explain a great many central elements of IR, and for that reason we cannot merely rest content treating them *as if* they were persons or treating their personality as a fiction; they *must* be real persons to do the things they are purported to do. While remaining agnostic about the ontological issues, I cannot agree with Wendt's attributions of agency and intention to states.

A fascinating alternative basis for asserting the *moral* personality of the state has been suggested by Amy Eckert in a series of recent essays.[97] Eckert relies upon the work of John Rawls, utilizing the criteria he set out for the constitution of moral personality, and applying those criteria to states. As distilled by Eckert, there are two criteria for the possession of moral personality, a conception of the good, "manifested in a rational life plan," and a sense of justice.[98] These were criteria Rawls designed for and applied to individuals; Eckert extends them by a series of analogies to states to assert the moral personality of states, asserting that it is "not allegorical, but real."[99] Rawls demonstrated his willingness to extend these criteria to a variety of *corpora,* although he did not specifically enumerate the state among them (he did, however, include "nations"). There are problems with this application of Rawls's thought that cause it the same problems as the other approaches so far surveyed. Eckert's approach, like all the others rests on a series of analogies. "States can possess the two powers associated with moral personality—the possession of a conception of the good and a sense of justice—albeit in a [somewhat] different form than natural persons."[100] In lieu of a rational life plan, societies (note the shift from "state") are organized around values. Standing in for the sense of justice is their reciprocal willingness to "limit the interests that they pursue to their reasonable...interests." She then takes the same turn as Wendt and Erskine and (without specific invocation of French) postulates a CIDS as the requisite "mechanism for deliberation" for the state's reflection upon and revision of its conception of the good. "States possess institutions and processes that allow them to deliberate and make decisions and are, therefore, the functional equivalents of these abilities that individuals possess...states can reflect on and even modify their conception of the good over time just as individuals can."[101] This approach, although it has much to commend it, ultimately falls prey to the same problems of reliance on analogy and metaphor that condemn French and the other corporate realists.

In the end, it comes to this: if we cannot attribute intention to the state, we cannot hold it criminally liable (wrongs of strict liability not requiring intention imputed to it via the rule *respondeat superior* will be addressed below). When we question the viability of the very language of the state acting, of attributing reason(s) to it, and the validity of speaking of its interests, there is no longer any conceptual foundation upon which to posit intentionality and hence criminal responsibility. It is too much to expect of a metaphor, a construct that Kelsen reminds us is only a "thinking aid," that it act, that it have reasons, beliefs, and desires, and that these sum to intentions. Even if we accept the trope of the state acting, it acts on the behalf of those who make it up and control its apparatus; *they* have reasons, beliefs and desires, and *they* act intentionally, but they are not the state, and their actions even in the aggregate are the state's only figuratively. They are responsible for their acts and for the acts of those who act upon their behalf (command responsibility), but the state, the collectivity (practically speaking, the people) cannot be reasonably held blameworthy for the actions of the individuals or groups directing things. It is, as Kelsen said, only "If . . . the state is considered as a real being, a kind of superman, the *illusion* is created that the sanctions provided by international law are directed against the same individual who has violated the law, in other words, we have the *illusion* of the individuality of the state as an international person."[102]

If we accept the conclusion that fictional entities with only fictional minds cannot form intentions (or that they form them only fictively), then the question of the tenability of *any* attributions of state responsibility arises. This is not a problem because we can still accept the utility of the Act of State Doctrine without the metaphysical baggage—at least in cases of strict liability (i.e., where there is no requirement of intent, only causation) through the use of the rule *respondeat superior*. Whether or not the state exists as any more than a legal fiction, when the acts of specified classes of individuals are conventionally attributable to the state in cases where fault does not require the intent to violate the law, it seems that at least delictual responsibility is tenable. This still does not support taking the next step unless a great deal more is stipulated.

The Stakes

The necessary stipulations referred to previously are legal and political questions, and turn us to practical questions: what is the utility of criminalizing the *state's* actions above and beyond that of the individuals who planned, ordered, carried out or abetted the actions? The utility issue is rhetorical, but the demand itself betrays a historical blindness. The demand for the criminalization of state acts returns us to the old dynamic of international punishment as advocated by *inter alia* Gentili, Grotius and Locke. Then, in the absence of the conceptual category of "the state," the nation (*gens*), effectively the populace, was punished for perceived violations of the Natural Law of nations. With the developments signaled in Hobbes, Pufendorf and Vattel, the state became the primary actor, and because it was recognized as sovereign it was rendered above the judgment of any of its peers. By focusing the law upon an imaginary entity that was immune from judgment or sanction, no one was subject to punishment for the violation of the fundamental (but no longer natural) laws of international society. When we rejected this in 1945 and demanded individual responsibility and liability for criminal(ized) actions, we made a major advance: from holding the entire populace responsible for the actions of some, to holding no one responsible, to holding the actual materially responsible parties liable. The demand to criminalize state behavior seen in the work of Anthony Lang and Jørgensen seems a remarkable leap backward. In one terminological respect this advocacy of punishing state criminality is an improvement on the Hobbes—1945 epoch, because it does represent recognition that no matter whom we consider to be the relevant actor, there are certain behaviors that will not be tolerated, and that no status confers immunity from judgment; sovereignty is not a shield. This does not, however, call for state criminalization in addition to individual criminal liability. Without accepting some sort of belief that the citizenry of the state collectively forms collective intentions upon which the state as the embodiment of the citizenry acts, and that the entirety of the population bears an aliquot share of the responsibility, there is no normative (or theoretical) justification for this reassertion of international punishment in its classical form.[103] Jørgensen sees little reason for concern on this ground, asserting contentedly "the implications of the term 'collective punishment' ought not, perhaps, to be exaggerated."[104] Lang, following Grotius's admonition, "Guilt attaches to the individuals who have agreed to the crime, not to those who have been overmastered by the votes of others," is less blasé about collective punishment, but does not rule out the punishment of whole societies, and regards the ILC's deletion of Article 19 as a signal failure of nerve.[105] If the sanction for states committing crimes is international sanctions in our more general sense of the term, it can be nothing other than collective punishment. If "smart" or targeted sanctions are put into place, designed to harm only certain parties while leaving the general populace unharmed, then the *state* is not being punished, only the leadership, and we are then led right back to individual liability and have no need to speak of state crimes.

Although the desire to ensure accountability for large scale crimes and to see to it that the perpetrators are punished for those crimes is surely understandable, the additional steps of punishing entire states is supportable neither in theoretical terms nor as a matter of ethics. Although many of the changes from the normative complex underlying classical international punishment have proved undesirable, a return to punishing entire societies because notional entities cannot be punished without punishing natural persons ultimately seems perverse.

CHAPTER 7

Conclusion

In early modern international society, Natural Law stood in for what we now call *jus cogens*. Its prohibitions were not only categorical, but also justified and perhaps even mandated a wide right of enforcement in the form of international punishment. Growing political dissatisfaction with the practice of international punishment and parallel philosophical dissatisfaction with its predicate basis in Natural Law led to the supplanting of these peremptory norms with new ones: absolute sovereignty, sovereign equality, and nonintervention. When in the mid-twentieth century these norms were presented as shields behind which to perpetrate genocides, this led to the displacement of these norms as peremptory by new norms. These new norms prohibit unconditionally acts that were considered the sovereign prerogatives of states in the previous era; these proscribed acts—it is now claimed—generate a universal right (and perhaps universal obligation) to prevent and punish their commission. They are prohibited at all times and under all circumstances, and are thus *jus cogens*. We also have a subsidiary category of norms that plays a similar role, obligations *erga omnes*. They differ from *jus cogens* in potentially allowing violation in some circumstances, and are thus not peremptory, but they share with *jus cogens* the generation of a right for any state, whether it is directly affected or not, to take legal action to ensure compliance under specified conditions still tied to Positivist Voluntarism. Formerly it was claimed that Natural Law trumped sovereignty; now international society holds that there are some nonderogable but positive obligations that trump sovereignty and trump any other obligations.

I regard these other developments as progressive, and as significant improvements over their conceptual precursor, international punishment. Grotian, Natural Law-based punishment entailed the imposition and enforcement of alien norms as a pretext for conquest; *jus cogens* and obligations *erga omnes,* because part of the Voluntarist Positive Law—even though not fully consensual in the case of *jus cogens*—are not acts of imposition, but rather give rise to *actiones populares* to enforce universal norms that trump sovereignty. These remain tentative developments, however, and we have already seen ways in which universal jurisdiction and the *actio popularis* are being challenged; so although it may be too soon to make the claim that international society has changed in fundamental ways, it is clear that the fundamental rules that have characterized it since the time of Vattel are facing challenges, and that something new may be in the process of formation.

Much remains inchoate. The claims of enthusiasts aside, it remains clear that a purported violation of a *jus cogens* obligation will not automatically give simply any party the standing to take legal measures. The case is the same with regard to the violation of obligations *erga omnes;* there is no immediate or necessary basis for an *actio popularis* under the current congeries of procedural norms. This presents what is on its face a curious anomaly: there is on the one hand, a set of norms that is considered peremptory and that should therefore be indefeasible which is effectively being trumped by other norms that are (merely) procedural. Closer analysis reveals this not to be the anomaly it appears; the procedural norms are, in fact, operational rules of the still-present absolute sovereignty normative complex. That is why the newer normative complex remains inchoate; it has not fully succeeded in supplanting its predecessor, and it is not altogether clear that the will or desire to do so is yet manifest.

To return to the conceptualization of change in categorical obligation utilized in the Introduction, we may be in a period in which a new final vocabulary is still developing, or a period in which it has developed, but has not yet displaced its own predecessor. As an empirical matter, there is no immediate way to disentangle these options, but it is of no moment; what matters is that the older final vocabulary and its attendant normative complex and practices remain in place, albeit under growing strain and increasing challenge. The more interesting question relates to the source of the putative new final vocabulary. The roots are clear enough: the revulsion engendered by the horrors segments of humanity have inflicted upon one another throughout the last seven decades, the frustration growing out of the impunity of many of the perpetrators and orchestrators. Clearly, however, the revulsion and condemnation are not universal as the practices recur with dismaying frequency. Nonetheless, returning to the characterization in the Introduction, by engaging in these practices and shielding those who engage in them (one is hard pressed to find *per se* advocates or defenders of these practices rather than apologists) these parties exclude themselves from the relevant moral "we," and from the moral community participating in the construction of the new final moral vocabulary. What remains to be seen is which group will carry the day.

In the coming years, as the ICC begins to see more cases, universal jurisdiction as a principle may gain strength and continue to challenge those residual forms of immunity associated with absolute notions of sovereignty. Conversely, however, we may encounter mounting resistance to the work of the ICC as we do with the recent Arab and African reaction to the al-Bashir indictment, and we are particularly likely to witness resistance to individual states attempting to exercise universal jurisdiction. Either dynamic may lead to the weakening of the nascent norm, and the strengthening of the older norm. In like manner, the issue of piracy off the coast of Africa is bringing questions of universal jurisdiction forward, although there seems to be a rather widespread amnesia with regard to the existence of universal standing to try and to punish pirates.

Although the transition to a new normative complex remains incomplete, its outlines are already quite clear. One area of contention, however, remains the scope and breadth of the right to punish. The most pressing matter in this regard is the revival of interest in, and assertions of, the right to punish entire states. As discussed in the previous chapter, there are both conceptual-theoretical problems with this revival and pressing normative problems. Unlike the modes of punishment or descendants of modes of punishment talked about in chapters 3 through 5, reviving the practice of punishing entire states, and by necessity entire nations, is most undesirable.

Notes

Chapter 1

1. Gerry Simpson, *Great Powers and Outlaw States: Unequal Sovereigns in the International Legal Order* (Cambridge: Cambridge University Press, 2004), 51.
2. Nicholas Greenwood Onuf, "The Constitution of International Society" *European Journal of International Law* 5 (1999): 1–19.
3. H. L. A. Hart, *The Concept of Law* 2nd ed. (Oxford: Oxford University Press, 1961 [1997]), 79–99.
4. "Secondary rules are all concerned with the primary rules themselves. They specify the ways in which the primary rules may be conclusively ascertained, introduced, eliminated, varied, and the fact of their violation conclusively determined." Hart (1961), 94.
5. Both "Positivism" and "Voluntarism" are terribly vexed terms; as they will figure prominently throughout, some preliminary clarification is in order. As it will be used here, Positivism refers generally to its usage in legal theory; in that context, it denotes laws that have been set out—posited—by human lawmakers, rather than being intrinsic to the natural order (Natural Law) or ordained by god (Divine Law). Having been posited, there will always be some form or another of evidence of the law and its content. Positivism also tends toward a separation of law and ethics—again in distinction from naturalism. "Voluntarism," as it is used in international law, is related doctrinally to Positivism; it holds that legal obligation over an agent can only be created by the consent of that agent, that is, for a state to be legally bound it must have consented (willed) to be bound. On the term's usage in ethics, see J. B. Schneewind, *The Invention of Autonomy* (Cambridge: Cambridge University Press, 1998), 8–9, 21–36, 95–100; Knud Haakonssen, *Natural Law and Moral Philosophy* (Cambridge: Cambridge University Press, 1996), 19–23, 45–51, 66–71.

6. Höffe uses the term "categorical principle" in a slightly different context. Ottfried Höffe, *Categorical Principles of Law*, trans. Mark Migotti (University Park: Penn State Press, 2002).

7. Immanuel Kant, *Groundwork for the Metaphysics of Morals* (1785), 4: 414–421.

8. *Vienna Convention on the Law of Treaties* 1155 U.N.T.S. 331, UN Doc. A/CONF.39/27 (1969).

9. This understanding comports up to a point with Kelsen's idea of the *Grundnorm*. He does not attribute peremptory status to the *Grundnorm*, but assigns it a more narrow functional role. Hans Kelsen, *Pure Theory of Law* 2nd ed. (Clark: The Lawbook Exchange, Ltd., 2005 [1967]), 8, 193–195.

10. On the circumstances precluding wrongfulness for violating an international obligation see the *Articles on the Responsibility of States for Internationally Wrongful Acts* (2001), Articles 20–26; Lauri Hannikainen, *Peremptory Norms in International Law* (Helsinki: Finnish Lawyers' Publishing Company, 1988), 249–257.

11. Richard Rorty, *Contingency, Irony and Solidarity* (Cambridge: Cambridge University Press, 1989), 73.

12. The imposition of indemnities—particular upon the state or states losing a war—remained a punitive practice into the twentieth century, but one lacking the normative basis of traditional international punishment.

13. The term "personate" comes from Hobbes. See Chapter 6.

14. There is a strand of contemporary international punishment that does involve the punitive use of force; the matter is expertly discussed in Anthony F. Lang, *Punishment, Justice and International Relations: Ethics and Order After the Cold War* (London: Routledge, 2008).

Chapter 2

1. See *inter alia* F. H. Hinsley, *Sovereignty* 2nd ed. (Cambridge: Cambridge University Press, 1986); Nicholas Greenwood Onuf, "Sovereignty, Outline of a Conceptual History," *Alternatives* 16 (1991): 425–446 (reprinted in expanded version in Onuf, *The Republican Legacy in International Thought* (Cambridge: Cambridge University Press, 1998), 113–138; Jens Bartelson, *A Genealogy of Sovereignty* (Cambridge: Cambridge University Press, 1995); Hideaki Shinoda, *Re-Examining Sovereignty: From Classical Theory to the Global Age* (New York: St. Martin's Press, 2000); R. B. J. Walker, *Inside/Outside: International Relations*

as Political Theory (Cambridge: Cambridge University Press, 1993), 153–183; Thomas J. Biersteker and Cynthia Weber, *State Sovereignty as Social Construct* (Cambridge: Cambridge University Press, 1996); Richard Ashley, "Untying the Sovereign State: A Double Reading of the Anarchy Problematique," *Millennium* 17 (1988): 227–262; Daniel Philpott, *Revolutions in Sovereignty: How Ideas Shaped Modern International Relations* (Princeton: Princeton University Press, 2001); Hendryk Spruyt, *The Sovereign State and its Competitors: An Analysis of Systems Change* (Princeton: Princeton University Press, 1994): 151–180; Michael Ross Fowler and Julie Marie Bunck, *Law Power and the Sovereign State: The Evolution and Application of the Concept of Sovereignty* (University Park: The Pennsylvania State University Press, 1996); Alan James, *Sovereign Statehood: The Basis of International Society* (London: Allen and Unwin, 1986); John Hoffman, *Sovereignty* (Minneapolis: University of Minnesota Press, 1998); Wouter G. Werner and Jaap H. de Wilde, "The Endurance of Sovereignty," *European Journal of International Relations* 7 (2001): 283–313; Andreas Osiander, "Sovereignty, International Relations and the Westphalian Myth," *International Organization* 55 (2001): 251–287.

2. Cynthia Weber, *Simulating Sovereignty* (Cambridge: Cambridge University Press, 1995), 11–29.

3. Hugo Grotius, *De Jure Belli ac Pacis.* II.I.II. Emphasis added.

4. Benjamin Straumann, " 'Ancient Caesarian Lawyers' in a State of Nature: Roman Tradition and Natural Rights in Hugo Grotius' *De Jure Praedae*," *Political Theory* 34/3 (2006b), 328–350; Benjamin Straumann, "Is Modern Liberty Ancient? Roman Remedies and Natural Rights in Hugo Grotius' Early Works on Natural Law," *International Law and Justice Working Papers* 2006/11 (2006c), 1–35. Hoag demonstrates similarly the way in which Grotius relied heavily on Augustine—not noting the latter's reliance on Roman jurisprudence. Robert Hoag, "The Recourse to War as Punishment: A Historical Theme in Just War Theory," *Studies in the History of Ethics* 2 (2006): 5–8.

5. When discussing Grotius, I use "nation" rather than "state" for a number of reasons: it is not clear that the Latin terms he used carried the full signification of our modern term. Writing in Latin, he used *civitas* and its cognates, *communis* and its cognates, *respublica* and its cognates, and *gentium*. Translations of Grotius do not agree with each other, and are internally inconsistent in the translation of these terms; sometimes a term is rendered "state," sometimes "nation," at other times "country,"

and even occasionally "commonwealth." Some of the problem lies in Grotius's text itself; it is not always clear contextually whether he sought to signify different things with the differing Latin terms, or if he was using them simply as synonyms. Although Goebel presents an impressive argument in favor of Grotius having a full-fledged conception of the sovereign state—or at least of such an idea being available to him in legal and diplomatic practice, if not doctrine—there remains little evidence for such in the text itself. Finally, as Goebel notes, in cases in which Grotius is referring to their relations with one another, instead of a term like *civitas,* he prefers *gentium*—a word well established as equivalent to nation—*princeps,* referring to the sovereign of the state, or *populus,* indicating the people. We will see a similar problem with the concept of "sovereignty" in Grotius *infra.* Goebel, "The Equality of States part 3," *Columbia Law Review* 23 (1923): 266–271.

6. *De Jure Belli ac Pacis.* II.XX.XL.1. Quoted also in Tuck, 102–103.

7. Grotius, however, did allow that ignorance might mitigate and *possibly* even exculpate guilt. The range of those to whom he might have extended this consideration was presumably extraordinarily narrow. *De Jure Belli ac Pacis.* II.XX.XLIII.2.

8. Hoag, 15.

9. *De Jure Praedae Commentarius,* XII. 274.

10. Tuck, 86, quoting Grotius, *De Jure Praedae Commentarius,* I, 21.

11. *De Jure Belli ac Pacis,* II.XX.VII.5; II.XX.IX.1–2; II.XX.XII.1. Tuck, 82 also quotes from Grotius's *De Jure Praede:*

> Is not the power to punish essentially a power that pertains to the state? Not at all! On the contrary, just as every right of the magistrate comes to him from the state, so has the same right come to the state from private individuals . . . since no one is able to transfer a thing that he never possessed, it is evident that the right of chastisement was held by private persons before it was held by the state.

Grotius, *De Jure Praede,* 91–92.

12. Straumann, "The Right to Punish as a Just Cause of War in Hugo Grotius' Natural Law," *Studies in the History of Ethics* 2 (2006a): 7.

13. Straumann (2006a), 5.

14. *Digest,* 50.17.54, quoted in Straumann (2006a), 6. On page 8, Straumann notes that the right to punish has not passed from the individual's hands completely; it is retained residually in situations in which there is no government present. This is noted as well by

Brown. Chris Brown, *Sovereignty, Rights and Justice: International Political Theory Today* (Cambridge: Polity Press, 2002), 30–31.

15. On reprisal see *De Jure Belli ac Pacis,* III.II *passim.*

16. Tuck, 88; Straumann (2006a), 8, 12–14.

17. Straumann (2006a), 10.

18. *De Jure Belli ac Pacis,* II.XX.XL.3.

19. *De Jure Belli ac Pacis,* II.XX.XLIV, II.XX.XLVIII, and II.XX. XLVII.4, respectively.

20. In this Grotius also broke with some of his more recent predecessors such as Suarez. John Finnis, "The Ethics of War and Peace in the Catholic Natural Law Tradition," in Terry Nardin, ed., *The Ethics of War and Peace: Secular and Religious Perspectives* (Princeton: Princeton University Press, 1996), 21.

21. *De Jure Belli ac Pacis,* III.VIII, III.XV (subsidiary discussions at III.IV, III.V, III.VI, III.XI–XIII.

22. *De Jure Praedae,* XII. 271.

23. *De Jure Belli ac Pacis,* II.XXI.I–II.

24. *De Jure Praedae,* XII. 272–273.

25. Maritain captures the matter nicely:

> Just as the words *poliz* or *civitas* are often translated by "state" (though the most appropriate name is "commonwealth" or "body politic," not "state"), so the words *principatus* and *suprema potestas* are often translated by "sovereignty" and the words *kurioz* or *princeps* ("ruler") by "sovereign." This is a misleading translation, which muddles the issue from the start. *Principatus* ("principality") and *suprema potestas* ("supreme power") simply mean "highest ruling authority," not sovereignty.

Maritain, "The Concept of Sovereignty," *American Political Science Review* 44 (1950): 344.

26. Goebels goes on to claim that Grotius "had a clear notion of the state as the possessor of sovereignty," but his invocation of the passage cited immediately *supra* is hardly as definitive as he supposes. Goebels, 270. Tuck asserts of a strong notion of sovereignty in Grotius as well. Tuck, 82, 96.

27. Tuck, 158.

28. Tuck, 159.

29. Tuck, 161.

30. Tuck, 171–180; cf. Farr, "Locke, Natural Law, and New World Slavery," *Political Theory* 36 (2008): 500–504.

31. John Locke, *Second Treatise of Government,* §7. Also quoted in part in Tuck, 170–171 and in Straumann (2006a): 13.

32. *Second Treatise,* §8.
33. Alex Tuckness, "Punishment, Property and the Limits of Altruism: Locke's International Asymmetry," *American Political Science Review* 102 (2008): 477.
34. Torbjørn Knutsen, *A History of International Relations Theory* 2nd ed. (Manchester: Manchester University Press. 1997), 90–92.
35. *Majestas,* or its English rendering, "majesty," plays an important role in Onuf's account of the conceptual history of sovereignty. Onuf (1998), 119, 126–130.
36. Gottfried Willhelm Leibniz, *Caeserinus Fürstenerius,* in Patrick Riley, ed., *Leibniz: Political Writings* (Cambridge: Cambridge University Press 1988), 113.
37. Riley, "Introduction" (quoting Leibniz, *Entrétiens de Philarete et d'Eugène,* F de C VI, p. 347), 27.
38. "Thus it can happen that another in our territory has the right of hunting, the right of mining, of hiring, of taxes; perhaps even the right of supreme jurisdiction or the right of judging capital crimes and exacting the penalty from condemned men, or even what is called the right of last instance, or the right to be appealed to over him who has territorial hegemony." Leibniz, *Caeserinus Fürstenerius,* in Riley, ed., 116.
39. Leibniz, *Caeserinus Fürstenerius,* in Riley, ed., 114.
40. Leibniz, *Caeserinus Fürstenerius,* in Riley, ed., 116.
41. Knutsen, 91.
42. Riley, ed., 27.
43.
> In addition to internal power and freedom, the possession of . . . sovereignty required sufficient consequence and influence to participate in European affairs . . . such a sovereignty would be in respect to other legal subjects on a basis of parity in the enjoyment of rights, irrespective of the size of its territory . . . the possession of external sovereignty itself established equal legal capacity. Goebel, 275–276.

44. Christian Wolff, *Jus Gentium Methodo Scientificum Pertractum* (1749), *Prolegomena* §§4–6.
45. Wolff (1749), §§22–25.
46. Wolff (1749), §§2.
47. Wolff (1749), §§7–15.
48. Wolff (1749), §§16–18.
49. Wolff (1749), §§13, 15.
50. Tuck, 191, citing Wolff (1749), §258.
51. Tuck, 190.

52. Tuck, 192, citing Emer Vattel, *Le Droit des Gens, ou Principes de la Loi Naturelle, Appliqués à la Conduite et aux Affaires des Nations et des Souverains* (1758). 9a. Onuf (1998), 77–81.

53. Tuck, 194, citing Vattel, 131 (II.IV. §54). See also Vattel, Introduction, §18.

54. Vattel, II.VII.73.

55. Vattel, Introduction, §§24–27.

56. Simpson (2004), 62–131.

57. Thomas Hobbes, *Leviathan* (1651), I.XVI. Samuel Pufendorf, *De Jure Naturae et Gentium Libro Octo* (1672). I.1.12. Vattel, Introduction, §§2, 4, 15, 16, 18–20; I.I.§1, 4; II.III. §35, 36.

58. Vattel, Introduction, §§18–20; II.IV. §54, 55; an even more rigid line is taken by Hegel in *Elements of the Philosophy of Right* (1821).

59. Distillation from Baker, "The Doctrine of Legal Equality of States," *British Yearbook of International Law* 4 (1923): 11.

60. Lassa Oppenheim, *International Law* 2nd ed. Volume 1 (New York: Longmans 1912), 169. Quoted in Baker, 12.

61. Simpson (2004), 28.

62. Hans Kelsen, "The Principle of Sovereign Equality of States as a Basis for International Organization," *Yale Law Journal* 53 (1944): 209. Simpson calls this the "principle of consent." Simpson (2004), 28.

63. There are holes in this, obviously, such as the principle that new states are "born" fully encumbered by existing customary legal obligations to which they never had the opportunity to consent or object. Michael Byers, *Custom, Power and the Power of Rules* (Cambridge: Cambridge University Press 1999), 77–78; Sir Humphrey Waldock, "General Course on Public International Law," *Recueil des Cours* 106 (1962) 49–53.

64. Simpson, 48, 51.

65. Vattel, Introduction, §§16, 20, 21.

66. G. W. F. Hegel, *Philosophy of Right,* §§333–334.

67. Baker, 6.

68. Kelsen (1944), 208.

69. John Westlake, *International Law Part 1: Peace* 1st ed. (Buffalo: W. S. Hein, 1910 (2000), 308). Quoted in Baker, p. 4. Fowler and Bunck reach much the same conclusion: "Thus sovereignty came to denote the independence of a state interacting in a system of states." Fowler and Bunck, 5.

70. Yoram Dinstein, "Par in Parem non Habet Imperium" *Israel Law Review* 1 (1966): 408.

71. Ernst H. Kantorowicz, *The Kings Two Bodies: A Study in Medieval Political Theology* (Princeton: Princeton University Press 1957), 452, n. 4.
72. Dinstein, 409.
73. Goebel, "The Equality of States, part 2," 129–130. The concept of the "political body" will be extensively analyzed in Chapter 6.
74. Goebel, "The Equality of States, part 2," 140.
75. Goebel, "The Equality of States, part 2," 140–141.
76. Dinstein, 413. A note of caution is warranted with this definition's importation of elements of the concept *potestas* to the definition of *imperium;* the former originally (despite the literal meaning of "power") connoting something closer to authority, and the latter, carrying from its military origins, the power to command and coerce. Hans Julius Wolff, *Roman Law* (Norman: University of Oklahoma Press, 1982), 27–29. We will return to this topic in the next chapter.
77. Robert Phillimore, *Commentaries Upon International Law* vol. 3. (Littleon: Fred B. Rothman and Co., 1857 (1985)), IX.II.VIII.
78. Westlake, 434. Quoted in Arnold D. McNair, "The Legal Meaning of War and the Relation of War to Reprisals," *Transactions of the Grotius Society* 11 (1925): 36.
79. Derek Bowett, "Reprisals Involving Recourse to Armed Force," *American Journal of International Law* 66 (1972): 3. Nearly identical descriptions are given in Tucker and Taulbee and Anderson. Robert W. Tucker, "Reprisals and Self-Defense: The Customary Law," *American Journal of International Law* 66 (1972): 589; James Larry Taulbee and John Anderson, "Reprisal *Redux,*" *Case Western Journal of International Law* 16 (1984): 312.
80. Further confusion is engendered by the multiple uses of the term "reprisal"; broadly speaking they might first be divided into "forcible" reprisals and "belligerent" reprisals. Forcible reprisal is the retaliatory / punitive use of force by one state against another for a violation of an international obligation that has not been redressed, and is thus subsumed under the *jus ad bellum.* Belligerent reprisals are a part of the *jus in bello.* They deal with reprisals by one belligerent against parties from their adversary (historically civilians or prisoners of war) for antecedent violations of the laws of armed conflict. Although not banned outright, the scope of belligerent reprisal has been greatly narrowed in the last century by a succession of treaties: Article 50 of the 1907 *Annex to Hague Convention IV Respecting the Laws and Customs of War on Land;* the 1929 *Geneva Convention Relative to the Treatment of Prisoners*

of War; Articles 16, 47, 13; and 33, respectively, of the four 1949 *Geneva Conventions.* Henry Wager Halleck, "Retaliation in War," *American Journal of International Law* 6 (1912): 107–118; Françoise J. Hampson, "Belligerent Reprisals and the 1977 Protocols to the Geneva Conventions of 1949," *International and Comparative Law Quarterly* 37 (1988): 818–843; Ingrid Detter, *The Laws of War* (Cambridge: Cambridge University Press 2000), 299–303; Philip Sutter, "The Continuing Role for Belligerent Reprisals," *Journal of Conflict and Security Law* 13 (2008): 93–122; Robert Kolb and Richard Hyde, *An Introduction to the Law of Armed Conflict* (Oxford: Hart Publishing 2008), 173–177.

81. Vattel, II.IV.51–52; he revisits the matter in nearly identical terms at II.IV.65–69.

82. List distilled from Lang (2008), 11–19.

83. This is the essence of belligerent reprisals.

84. But see Vattel, II.IV.51–52; II.IV.55; III.III.41 on reprisals.

85. Theodore D. Woolsey, *Introduction to the Study of International Law* 4th (Littleton: Fred B. Rothman and Co., 1871 (1999), 174. Emphasis in original. Kelly, 4–5 quotes some of this passage from a different edition of Woolsey.

86. Wilhelm G. Grewe, *The Epochs of International Law,* Michael Byers, trans. (New York: de Gruyter 2000), 201.

87. It is noteworthy that Wolff held the right to engage in reprisal to be limited strictly to nations. Wolff (1749), §589.

88. Grover Clark, "The English Practice with Regard to Reprisals by Private Persons," *American Journal of International Law* 27 (1933): 694–723. Indeed, domestically reprisal could be carried out at the level of towns: "As late as the quarter of the 13th century, it was legal, in England, for the authorities of one town, on behalf of the private citizens of the town, to take reprisals on the citizens of another . . . It will be observed, however, that the reprisals were not taken by the private persons who had suffered, but by the authorities of the towns on behalf of those persons." Clark, 704–705.

89. Michael J. Kelly, "Time Warp to 1945—Resurrection of the Reprisal and Anticipatory Self-Defense Doctrines in International Law," *Journal of Transnational Law and Policy* 13 (2003): 4.

90. Kelly, 4.

91. Wolff treats the capture of individuals as part of reprisal under the heading of "androlepsy." While he does not allow captives of this sort to be killed if compensation is not forthcoming, he does permit their being "kept in prison forever as captives,

or where slavery is practiced, to become slaves." Wolff (1749), §§ 592–595.

92. Clark, 698.
93. Clark, 700–701.
94. Clark, 695–698; 720. As Woolsey presents the matter at p. 195:

> Every authority in those times could make war, could grant letters of reprisals. But when power began to be more centralized, the sovereign gave to magistrates, governors of provinces and courts the right of issuing them, until at length this right was reserved for the central government alone.

95. Kelly, 5.
96. Clark, 711.
97. Phillimore, IX.II.X.
98. Henry Wheaton, *Elements of International Law* (1866), IV.I.291. Also cited in Kelly, 5. Of reprisals of this type, an author only recorded as B. F. stated, "A commission of general reprisals is stronger than even a declaration of war, authorizing the seizure of the goods of the foreign subjects everywhere and immediately." B. F., "The International Law of Embargo and Reprisal," *Law Magazine or Quarterly Review of Jurisprudence* 24 (1840): 74.
99. Grewe, 369, 525.
100. Grewe, 203. Privateering (and its relation to piracy) will be discussed in more detail in Chapter 5.
101. Janice E. Thomson, *Mercenaries, Pirates and Sovereigns: State-Building and Extraterritorial Violence in Early-Modern Europe* (Princeton: Princeton University Press, 1994), 22–26.
102. Clark, 702. Emphasis in original.
103. Bowett analyzes a series of 20 reprisals involving Israel and its neighbors spanning the years 1953–1970, as well as a British action against Yemen, and Portuguese reprisals against Zambia, Senegal, and Guinea. Kelly looks more narrowly at the British Yemen reprisal, Israel's 1972 reprisals against Lebanon, its 1985 raid on Tunis, the 1986 U.S. action against Libya, and its 1988 reprisal against Iranian oil platforms. Bowett, 4–17, 33–36; Kelly, 14–19.
104. Falk offers a significantly more detailed list consisting of 12 items. Richard Falk, "The Beirut Raid and the International Law of Retaliation," *American Journal of International Law* 63 (1969): 441–442.
105. Tucker, 592; Taulbee and Anderson, 312.
106. Tucker, 593.

107. Tucker, 591–592; McDougal and Feliciano are noteworthy for holding the latter view, Myres S. McDougal and Florentino P. Feliciano, *Law and Minimum World Public Order* (New Haven: New Haven Press 1961), 682.

108. Taulbee and Anderson, 314.

109. Falk, 429; Bowett, 1–2; Tucker, 586–587; Taulbee and Anderson, 309–310; Jeffrey Allen McCredie, "The April 14, 1986 Bombing of Libya: Act of Self-Defense or Reprisal?," *Case Western Journal of International Law* 19 (1987): 237; Detter, 87–88; Kelly, 12–13.

110. Ian Brownlie, *International Law and the Use of Force by States* (Oxford: Oxford University Press 1963), 281. Quoted in Falk, 428.

111. *Legality of the Threat of Use of Nuclear Weapons,* Advisory Opinion of 8 July 1996, ¶ 46.

112. For an extended analysis of the raid on Libya as a reprisal, see McCredie, *passim.*

113. Although in his denunciation of sovereignty both "as a word and as a concept" Maritain puts this forward as a logical conclusion of the meaning of sovereignty in its international context, it is not a position he held. Maritain, 343, 355–356.

114. Wheaton, IV.I.290.

115. *Leviathan.* I.XVIII.7; John Austin, *The Province of Jurisprudence Determined* (New York: The Lawbook Exchange 1832 (1999)), 5–11.

116. Austin, 110–111; 132.

117. Hans Kelsen, "The Essence of International Law," in Leo Gross, Karl Deutsch & Stanley Hoffmann, eds., *The Relevance of International Law* (Cambridge, MA: Schenkman Publishing 1968), 85–89; see also Hans Kelsen, *Principles of International Law* (Clark, NJ: The Lawbook Exchange. 1952 (2003)), 19–25; Hans Kelsen, *Law and Peace in International Relations* (Buffalo: William S. Hein and Co. 1942 (1997)), 31–34; Simpson (2004), 64.

118. Kelsen (1968), 85–86.

Chapter 3

1. R. St. J. MacDonald, "Fundamental Norms in Contemporary International Law," *Canadian Yearbook of International Law* 25 (1987): 134.

2. Prosper Weil, "Towards Relative Normativity in International Law," *American Journal of International Law* 77 (1983). Weil's skepticism regarding hierarchies of norms—inspired in part by the

development of the concept of *jus cogens*—has led to a number of responses: Ulrich Fastenrath, "Relative Normativity in International Law," *European Journal of International Law* 4 (1993): 305–340; J. H. H Weiler and Andreas L. Paulus, "The Structure of Change in International Law or Is There is Hierarchy of Norms in International Law?" *European Journal of International Law* 8 (1997): 545–565; Martti Koskenniemi, "Hierarchy in International Law: A Sketch," *European Journal of International Law* 8 (1997): 566–582; Juan Antonio Carrillo Salcedo, "Reflections on the Existence of a Hierarchy of Norms in International Law," *European Journal of International Law* 8 (1997): 583–595; Jason Beckett, "Behind Relative Normativity: Rules and Process as Prerequisites of Law," *European Journal of International Law* 12 (2001): 627–650; Dinah Shelton, "Normative Hierarchy in International Law," *American Journal of International Law* 100 (2006): 291–323. The phrases "more binding" and "more imperative" are used in a different but related context in Grigory I. Tunkin, "*Jus Cogens* in Contemporary International Law," *University of Toledo Law Review* 3 (1971): 116.

3. "State practice cited in support of overriding norms of *jus cogens* seems suspect and fragmented." Gordon A. Christenson, "*Jus Cogens:* Guarding Interests Fundamental to International Society," *Virginia Journal of International Law* 28 (1988): 587.

4. Except where otherwise noted, the lexical and etymological information in this section comes from either the *Oxford English Dictionary* or the *Oxford Latin Dictionary*.

5. One also occasionally finds "compulsory" and "mandatory."

6. Gaius, *Institutes* IV.120–121.

7. Wolff (1982), 28. Emphasis added.

8. Nicholas Greenwood Onuf, *World of Our Making: Rules and Rule in Social Theory and International Relations* (Columbia: University of South Carolina Press, 1989), 87, 93, 211–212. In a later work, Onuf uses the verb "demand" as exemplary. Nicholas Greenwood Onuf, "Constructivism: A User's Manual," in Vendulka Kubálková et al., eds, *International Relations in a Constructed World* (Armonk: M.E. Sharpe, 1998), 66.

9. Kant, 4:416.

10. "Peremptory norms are not just binding but operate in an absolute and unconditional way." Alexander Orakhelashvili, *Peremptory Norms in International Law* (Oxford: Oxford University Press, 2006), 67.

11. "Anything that is granted to someone without legal compulsion counts as a gift." *Digest* 39.5.29. The translation is from *The*

Digest of Justinian, trans. Watson (College Station: University of Pennsylvania Press, 1998). Suy hastens to note that "this passage has nothing to do with the traditional notion of jus cogens" of international law. Erik Suy, "The Concept of Jus Cogens in Public International Law" in the Lagonissi Conference on International Law Papers and Proceedings II: The Concept of Jus Cogens in International Law (Geneva: Carnegie Endowment for International Peace (European Centre), 1967), 18.

12. "Public law cannot be discharged [changed] by private pacts." (Papinian) *Digest* 2.14.38; cited in Suy, 18 and Vladimir Paul, "Legal Consequences of Conflict Between a Treaty and an Imperative Norm of General International Law," *Österreichische Zeitschrift für Öffentliches Recht* 21 (1974): 20. Translation from Watson; the bracketed emendation is mine. Cf. *Digest* 50.17.45, *privatorum conventio juri publico non derogat; the agreement of private individuals does not derogate from public law*. Cited in Georg Schwarzenberger, "International Jus Cogens?" *Texas Law Review* 43 (1965): 456, n. 5; translation from Watson. Gaius asserted that since the Law of Solon (sixth century B.C.), anything that citizens "agree by themselves will be valid unless forbidden by public statutes." *Digest*, 47.22.4; cited in Suy, 19; translation from Watson.

13. Christenson, (1988), 631, 633.

14. Egon Schwelb, "Some Aspects of International *Jus Cogens* as formulated by the International Law Commission," *American Journal of International Law* 61 (1967): 948; Suy, p. 19; Levan Alexidze, "The Legal Nature of *Jus Cogens* in Contemporary International Law," *Recueil des Cours* 172 (1981): 233. Alexidze includes Savigny, Pukhta, Windcheid and Baron among the Pandectists. Alexidze, 234, 266, n. 23.

15. Schwarzenberger, 456–457; Schwelb, 948–949; Suy, 18–22; Paul, pp. 44–46; Christos L. Rozakis, *The Concept of Jus Cogens in the Law of Treaties* (New York: North-Holland Publishing Co., 1976), 1–2, n. 1; Alexidze, 233–242; Milenko Kreça, "Some General Reflections on Main Features of *Jus Cogens* as Notion of International Law" [*sic*] in Gutiérrez, et. al., *New Directions in International Law* (Frankfurt: Campus Verlag, 1982), 27; Christenson (1988): 597–602 (Christenson is deeply skeptical of the analogy); A. Mark Weisburd, "The Emptiness of the Category of *Jus Cogens*, as Illustrated by the War in Bosnia-Herzegovina," *Michigan Journal of International Law* 17 (1995): 25–27 (Weisburd is also strongly critical of the analogy); Alfred P. Rubin, "*Actio Popularis, Jus Cogens, and Offenses Erga Omnes?*" *New England Law Review* 35 (2001): 272–273; Orakhelashvili, 11–26.

16. Paul, 20; Karen Parker and Lyn Beth Neylon, "*Jus Cogens:* Compelling the Law of Human Rights," *Hastings International and Comparative Law Review* 12 (1989): 419–422.
17. Wolff, *Jus Gentium, Prolegomena,* §§4–6. Emphasis added.
18. Vattel, *Le Droit des Gens,* Introduction, §§7–9.
19. Christenson (1988): 612; Michael Byers "Conceptualizing the Relationship between *Jus Cogens* and *Erga Omnes* Rules," *Nordic Journal of International Law* 66 (1997): 224.
20. Alfred von Verdross, "Forbidden Treaties in International Law," *American Journal of International Law* 31 (1937): 571–577. Both Schwelb and MacDonald, however, credit the ILC's second Rapporteur at the Vienna Convention, Lauterpacht's 1953 "Report on the Law of Treaties" to the International Law Commission for the "doctrine's reappearance." Schwelb, 949; MacDonald, 29. As a *concept*, but without express invocation of the name, *jus cogens* was discussed by both Bluntschli and Hall in the nineteenth century. Paul, 20, n. 3, 4. Their formulations, especially Hall's, were clear precursors to Verdross's.
21. Verdross, 571–572. Rozakis's much later assessment of the orthodox doctrine is more blunt still: "States were unconditionally free to conclude agreements of whatever content, even if contrary to already general rules of law." Rozakis, 3. Janis shares their assessment. Mark W. Janis, "The Nature of *Jus Cogens,*" *Connecticut Journal of International Law* 3 (1988): 362; Rafael Nieto-Navia, "International Peremptory Norms (*Jus Cogens*) and International Humanitarian Law" www.iccnow.org/documents/WritingColumbiaeng.pdf 4.
22. The "General principles" formulation is from Article 38 (1)(c) of the *Statute of the International Court of Justice,* which corresponds to Article 38 (3) of the *Statute of the Permanent Court of International Justice,* Verdross's point of reference.
23. Verdross (1937): 574. Emphasis in original. His emphasis later changed; he subsequently came to include "all rules of general international law created for humanitarian purposes." Alfred Verdross, "*Jus Dispositivum* and *Jus Cogens* in International Law," *American Journal of International Law* 60 (1966): 59–60.
24. Verdross (1937): 574. Although the third and fourth functions have individuals as their objects, they do not entail restrictions on how a state may treat its own nationals.
25. Under the rules of the *Vienna Convention* (Art. 44, ¶5), however, the treaty in its entirety would be void.
26. Verdross (1937): 577.

27. Sir Ian Sinclair, *The Vienna Convention on the Law of Treaties* 2nd ed. (Manchester: Manchester University Press, 1984), 224, cited in Christenson (1988): 591.

28. "Some states or writers maintain that it has been imposed on states as a consequence of natural law, having its source in human nature or emanating from a divine source and so being independent of the will of states." Paul, 29. Danilenko cites the statements of several of the states' representatives to the Vienna Conference that "stressed the fact that *jus cogens* derived its origin from concepts of natural law." Danilenko, 44, n. 7, 8.

    Although many representatives to the Vienna Conference may have been thinking of *jus cogens* in naturalist terms, it is clear from the report of the fourth Special Rapporteur Waldock that the International Law Commission "based its approach to the question of *jus cogens* on positive law much more than on natural law" when drafting the preliminary versions of what became Articles 53 and 64. Danilenko, 45, quoting Waldock from the proceedings of the Vienna Conference, volume I, p. 327. See also Lisa Yarwood, "*Jus Cogens:* Useful Tool or Passing Fancy? A Modest Attempt at Definition," *Bracton Law Journal* 38 (2006): 23–24.

29. Andrea Bianchi, "Human Rights and the Magic of *Jus Cogens,*" *European Journal of International Law* 19 (2008): 492.

30. Orakhelashvili details and dismisses the arguments of a number of dissenters from the general view. Orakhelashvili, 207–208. Tunkin concludes that the rule of Article 53 applies to customary rules as well as treaties. Tunkin, 117; Rozakis, 22.

31. Hannikainen, 6, 201. Emphasis in original.

    "If an international *jus cogens* exists it must, indeed, make necessarily null and void any of those legal acts and actions of States whose object is unlawful . . . Any legal act of whatever nature . . . is unlawful in so far as it infringes a rule of the *jus cogens* . . . one does not see why something which is intolerable as far as international treaties are concerned would not be so in respect of any other legal act." Suy, 75.

    "By its very nature, the notion of *jus cogens* goes beyond the law of treaties and makes itself relevant to the whole structure of international law." Ogawa, "International *Jus Cogens* Revisited," *Kwansei Gakuin Law Review* 12 (1986): 21. Cited in Hannikainen, 201.

32. ILC Report 1966, UN Doc A/6309/Rev. 1, p. 89; cited in Hannikainen, 7. Emphasis added. The ILC has maintained this position in its work on codifying the rules applicable to unilateral acts. Orakhelashvili, 208.

33. *Juridical Condition and Rights of Undocumented Migrants* (Advisory Opinion), ¶99, cited in Orakhelashvili, 207.
34. Orakhelashvili, 206.
35. Christenson (1988): 595, n. 35. The fact that he does not take note of the ILC's commentary must surely undermine his principal claim. Paulus also notes the primary rule character of the ILC's formulation. Andreas L. Paulus, "*Jus Cogens* in a Time of Hegemony and Fragmentation," *Nordic Journal of International Law* 74 (2005): 305. Kawasaki is more skeptical yet. Kyoji Kawasaki, "A Brief Note on the Legal Effects of *Jus Cogens* in International Law," *Hitotsubashi Journal of Law and Politics* 34 (2006): 31–35; Ulf Linderfalk, "The Effects of *Jus Cogens* Norms," *European Journal of International Law* 18 (2008): 856.
36. *United States Diplomatic and Consular Staff in Tehran* (U.S. v Iran), 1979. ¶88. As discussed, "imperative" may not be an exact synonym for "peremptory," but again, in the French text of the *Vienna Convention*, "imperative" is used in place of "peremptory," which adds weight to the conclusion that the Court in *Hostages* was treating the rules regarding the status of diplomatic persons and premises as *jus cogens*. Hannikainen, 192–193.
37. Case Concerning Military and Paramilitary Activities in and Against Nicaragua (Nicaragua v U.S.), 1986; Gordon A. Christenson, "The World Court and Jus Cogens," *American Journal of International Law* 81 (1987): 93–101; Christenson (1988): 607, 621, n. 152; Hannikainen, 5, 14, 192–194; Alexidze, 228; Giorgio Gaja, "Jus Cogens Beyond the Vienna Convention," *Recueil des Cours* 173 (1981): 285–286. Kadelbach offers a detailed list. Stefan Kadelbach, "Jus Cogens, Obligations Erga Omnes, and Other Rules—The Identification of Fundamental Norms" in Christian Tomuschat and Jean-Marc Thouvenin, eds, *The Fundamental Rules of the International Legal Order: Jus Cogens and Obligations Erga Omnes* (Leiden: Martinus Nijhoff Publishers, 2006), 32, n. 45.
38. *Armed Activities on the Territory of the Congo* (DRC v Rwanda) (New Application), 2002, ¶64; *Application of the Convention on the Prevention and Punishment of the Crime of Genocide* (Bosnia and Herzegovina v Serbia and Macedonia), 2007, ¶161.
39. *Prosecutor v Furundzija*, ¶114; also note the discussion at ¶153–156.
40. *Resolution 3/87, Case 9647*, ¶56. Cited in Christenson (1988): 608, 621–623.
41. Hannikainen, 3, 6.
42. Hannikainen, 207.

43. de Hoogh brazenly asserts, "To state that a norm is peremptory means that it is binding on all States alike, whether they are opposed to it or not." A. J. J. de Hoogh, "The Relationship Between *Jus Cogens,* Obligations *Erga Omnes* and International Crimes: Peremptory Norms in Perspective," *Austrian Journal of Public International Law* 42 (1991): 186.

44. In its preparatory work on international crimes and delicts for the *Articles on State Responsibility* (see Chapter 6), the ILC revisited the question of the meaning of "international community as a whole" stating, " 'It certainly does not mean the requirement of unanimous recognition by all members' of the international community; this would give each State a right of veto, which would be unthinkable." Hannikainen, 211; Orakhelashvili, 104–108.

45. Gaja, 283.

46. MacDonald, 130–131. This applies to *jus cogens per se,* not to the individual norms.

47. MacDonald, 136; de Hoogh, 86–187; Byers (1997): 217, 222, 227–228. The persistent objector rule is part of customary international law that holds that a state that objects consistently to a rule of customary law from the very time of its development will not become bound by that rule, whereas states that actively participate in the creation of the rule or states that remain passive in the face of the developing rule will be subject to that rule. On the persistent objector rule, see the *Asylum Case* (Colombia v Peru) ICJ 1957; Michael Akehurst, "Custom as a Source of International Law," *British Yearbook of International Law* 47 (1976): 23–27; Ted L. Stein, "The Approach of the Different Drummer: The Principle of the Persistent Objector in International Law," *Harvard International Law Journal* 26 (1985): 457–482; Jonathan I. Charney, "The Persistent Objector Rule and the Development of Customary International Law," *British Yearbook of International Law* 56 (1985): 1–24; David A. Colson, "How Persistent Must the Persistent Objector Be?" *Washington Law Review* 61 (1986): 957–970; Karol Wolfke, *Custom in Present International Law* 2nd ed. (Dordrecht: Martinus Nijhoff Publishers, 1993), 66–67; Michael Byers, *Custom, Power and the Power of Rules: International Relations and Customary International Law* (Cambridge: Cambridge University Press, 1999), 180–183.

48. Kreça, 34. Turpel and Sands, conversely, explicitly invoke Rousseau's "general will," but reach the opposite conclusion: "The requirement of acceptance by the international community … obviously implies *consent* for peremptory norms." Mary Ellen

Turpel and Phillipe Sands, "Peremptory International Law and Sovereignty: Some Questions," *Connecticut Journal of International Law* 3 (1988): 365, 367; Jean Jacques Rousseau, *Discourse on Political Economy.* ¶12, 15, 16, 23, 58; *Social Contract* II.4.1, 5; IV.1.1. Rousseau, of course, denied that there was or could be a general will encompassing all of humanity. *Geneva Manuscript* I.2.8. A more direct parallel might be found in the work of Heinrich Triepel, who articulated a "doctrine of the common will of States as the basis of international law. The essence of this doctrine was that the will of individual states could not be the source of international law." Grewe, 505.

49. Danilenko, 50.

50. Hannikainen, 12; Linderfalk, 862.

51. Alexidze, 258. MacDonald provides a similar formulation. MacDonald, 130; Hannikainen, 4. Danilenko offers a caveat, however: "Dissenting states cannot succeed in preventing the formation of a rule of *jus cogens*. However, this does not necessarily imply the view that such rules will be opposable to them in cases when they persistently objected to the rules." Danilenko, 54.

52. Paulus offers some tentative answers. Paulus, 303.

53. Kreça's talk of "objective orders" comes close to naturalism. Kreça, 29.

54. Danilenko, 53; Nieto-Navia, 9.

55. Hannikainen, 208.

56. Nicholas Greenwood Onuf and Richard K. Birney, "Peremptory Norms of International Law: Their Source, Function and Future," *Denver Journal of International Law and Policy* 4 (1974): 190, n. 9.

57. In the preparatory work for the *Vienna Convention,* the ILC's Drafting Committee clearly indicated its sense that "general" indeed should be taken to mean "universal." Hannikainen, 209. "Universal" appears only in the Preamble with reference to "the principles of free consent and of good faith and the *pacta sunt servanda* rule" and to "respect for human rights and fundamental freedom for all," so Hannikainen's recourse to the Preamble seems inapposite.

58. Rozakis, 55.

59. Alexidze, 246.

60. Alexidze, 247.

61. Rorty (1989), 73.

I cannot agree with the assertion that the properties Rorty identifies in the second part of this quote are general properties of deontic language; to accept that position would mean that no "ought" statement can be justified noncircularly, and that there is no "distance" between the set of moral assertions that comprises our ethics and the primitives of our final vocabulary. For most of the statements to which we ascribe normativity, we do so not by direct reference to our moral simples, but we predicate them upon complex congeries of other interlocking norms. In practice, we defend the normativity of a practice, belief, or claim by reference to an antecedent, higher-order norm. Defending any deontic statement might yield a *regress* that would ultimately lead to the primitives of the final vocabulary, but that is not the same thing as saying that all deontic language and hence all "ought" statements are "as far as we can go with language."

62. Verdross (1966), 58.

63. Mexican representative to the Vienna Convention, quoted in Yarwood, 28.

64. Kreça, 31.

65. Rorty does not believe that "searches for a final vocabulary are destined to converge," but simply because they are not so destined does not mean that on some points they will not converge, or that it would be inappropriate to speak of suitably thin shared final vocabulary. Rorty (1989), 76.

This "we" is a very malleable referent that, in principle, extends from the individual to the whole of the international society. Although universally agreed upon norms are vanishingly rare, *jus cogens* has been defined in such a way as to negotiate this *aporia,* and as reference to the debates surrounding the inclusion of peremptory norms in the Vienna Convention indicates, support was nearly universal, and representative of all cultural, political, economic, and religious groupings.

On the breadth of support for the inclusion of such norms, see Hannikainen, 145–180. MacDonald highlights the "insistent support of the Asian, African and Latin American States," which were "primarily concerned with the values the international order embraced; in particular they wanted to use the doctrine as a tool to achieve economic and political equality with the West." MacDonald, 129–130; Alexidze, 230. Tunkin emphasizes the support from both sides of the Cold War ideological divide. Tunkin, 110.

66. Kreça, 28.

67. Myres McDougal and Michael Reisman, "The Prescribing Function in the World Constitutive Process: How International Law is

Made," in Myres McDougal and Associates, eds, *International Law Essays* (New York: The Foundation Press, 1981), 373.

68. Onuf and Birney, 196–197.

69. Richard Rorty, *Philosophy and Social Hope* (New York: Penguin Books, 1999), 83; Ludwig Wittgenstein, *Philosophical Investigations* 3rd ed. (1958), ¶217. "If I have exhausted the justifications I have reached bedrock, and my spade is turned. Then I am inclined to say: 'This is simply what I do.' "

70. Rorty (1989), 80.

71. This usage of "thin" comes from Michael Walzer, *Thick and Thin: Moral Argument at Home and Abroad* (Notre Dame: University of Notre Dame Press, 1994), 1–19, 61–84. On the "Cosmopolitan—Communitarian Debate" see Chris Brown, *International Relations Theory: New Normative Approaches* (New York: Columbia University Press, 1992) 23–77; Charles Jones, *Global Justice: Defending Cosmopolitanism* (Oxford: Oxford University Press, 1999); Molly Cochran, *Normative Theory in International Relations: A Pragmatic Approach* (Cambridge: Cambridge University Press, 1999) 21–77.

72. See *inter alia,* Karl Llewellyn, "A Realistic Jurisprudence—The Next Step," *Columbia Law Review* 30 (1930): 431–465; Karl Llewellyn, "Some Realism about Realism," *Harvard Law Review* 44 (1931): 1222–1264; Hessel Yntema, "American Legal Realism in Retrospect," *Vanderbilt Law Review* 14 (1960): 317–330; William Fisher III et al., eds., *American Legal Realism* (Oxford: Oxford University Press, 1993); Harry D. Gould and Nicholas Greenwood Onuf, "Pragmatism, Legal Realism and Constructivism," in Harry Bauer and Elisabetta Brighi, eds., *Pragmatism in International Relations* (London: Routledge, 2009), 32–38.

73. By contrast, Schwarzenberger sees *jus cogens* as nothing but morality clad in the language of law, "the alleged incompatibility of any particular treaty with international *jus cogens* provides splendid opportunities for the expression of moral indignation by third parties in a semi-legal jargon on matters which, otherwise, would clearly not be their business." Schwarzenberger, 477.

74. "Rules may be stated in very general terms, in which case we might call it a principle." Onuf (1998), 67.

75. Richard Rorty, "Human Rights, Rationality and Sentiment," in Richard Rorty, ed., *Truth and Progress: Philosophical Papers* vol. 3 (Cambridge: Cambridge University Press, 1998), 177.

76. Rorty (1998), 177–178.

Chapter 4

1. Michael Byers, "Conceptualizing the Relationship Between *Jus Cogens* and *Erga Omnes* Rules," *Nordic Journal of International Law* 66 (1997): 238.
2. Christian Tams, *Enforcing Obligations Erga Omnes in International Law* (Cambridge: Cambridge University Press, 2005), 158.
3. Karl Zemanek, "New Trends in the Enforcement of *Erga Omnes* Obligations," *Max Planck Yearbook of United Nations Law* (2000): 8.
4. René Lefeber, "Cum Grano Salis," *Leiden Journal of International Law* 11 (1998): 5.
5. A. J. J. de Hoogh, *Obligations Erga Omnes and International Crimes: A Theoretical Inquiry into the Implementation and Enforcement of the International Responsibility of States* (Leiden: Martinus Nijhoff, 1996), 54.
6. Maurizio Ragazzi, *The Concept of International Obligations Erga Omnes* (Oxford: Oxford University Press (Clarendon Press), 1997); see also Kriangsak Kittichaisaree, *International Criminal Law* (Oxford University Press, 2001), 11–13; R. St. J. MacDonald, "Fundamental Norms in Contemporary International Law," *Canadian Yearbook of International Law* 25 (1987): 136–139; Olivia Lopez Pegna, "Counter-claims and Obligations Erga Omnes before the International Court of Justice," *European Journal of International Law* 9/4 (1998): 724–736; de Hoogh (1991).
7. Stefan Kadelbach "Jus Cogens, Obligations Erga Omnes, and Other Rules—The Identification of Fundamental Norms" in Christian Tomuschat and Jean-Marc Thouvenin, eds, *The Fundamental Rules of the International Legal Order: Jus Cogens and Obligations Erga Omnes* (Leiden: Martinus Nijhoff Publishers, 2006), 26; Christian Hillgruber, "The Right of Third States to Take Countermeasures" in Thomuschat and Thouvenin, eds, 265–294, *passim;* Tams, 198–249, *passim.*
8. M. Sherif Bassiouni, "Universal Jurisdiction for International Crimes: Historical Perspectives and Contemporary Practice," *Virginia Journal of International Law* 42 (2001): 88; see also William J. Aceves, "*Actio Popularis?* The Class Action in International Law," *University of Chicago Legal Forum* (2003): 398. On the Roman law roots of the concept, see J. A. van der Vyver, "*Actiones Populares* and the Problem of Standing in Roman, Roman-Dutch, South

African and American Law," *Acta Juridica* (1978): 191–193; Alfred P. Rubin, *"Actio Popularis, Jus Cogens,* and Offenses *Erga Omnes?"* *New England Law Review* 35 (2001): 268.

9. van der Vyver, 194–201.

10. van der Vyver, 191–192, n. 2, 3.

11. van der Vyver, 192.

12. Egon Schwelb, "The *Actio Popularis* and International Law," *Israel Yearbook on Human Rights* 2 (1972): 47, n. 6; van der Vyver, 192. Rubin's brusque dismissal of the *actio popul100aris* by associating it with slavery *simpliciter* is wholly unwarranted and indeed irresponsible. Rubin (2001), 268.

13. Aceves, 398.

14. Byers (1997), 238.

15. Tams discusses a number of subsidiary cases that will not be addressed here. Tams, 187–192.

16. Terry Gill, ed. *Rosenne's The World Court* 6th ed. (Leiden: Martinus Nijhoff Publishers, 2003), 138.

17. *South-West Africa (Liberia v. South Africa Ethiopia v. South Africa)* Application ¶4–8. ICJ 1966; Tams, 64; Schwelb, (1972): 47–49; Aceves, 356–357; Gill, ed. 137–142.

18. The relevant provision of the Mandate Agreement, Article 7(2), states: "The Mandatory agrees that, if any dispute whatever should arise between the Mandatory and another Member of the League of Nations relating to the interpretation or the application of the provisions of the Mandate, such dispute, if it cannot be settled by negotiation."

19. *South-West Africa* Preliminary Objections, 452. Note President Winiarski's incorrect attribution of the *actio popul100aris* to penal law rather than the law of obligations.

20. *South-West Africa* Preliminary Objections, 425. Also quoted in Tams, 51.

21. de Hoogh (1991), 194–195.

22. *South-West Africa* Judgment, ¶88, at 47.

23. *South-West Africa* Judgment, ¶88, at 47. Gill, ed. 140; Aceves, 356–367.

24. Schwelb rightly notes Justice Jessup's dissent that set the stage for later developments. Schwelb, 48, citing Jessup's separate opinion in the preliminary phase (1962) and his dissent in the Decision. de Hoogh asserts, however, that there was no basis in the text of the Mandate Agreement for Liberia and Ethiopia to make such a claim. de Hoogh (1991), 197.

25. Schwelb, 49–55.

26. Tams, 68.

27. *Case Concerning Barcelona Light, Power and Traction ltd. (Belgium v. Spain)* ICJ 1970, Summary of Judgment, 1.

28. *Case Concerning Barcelona Light, Power and Traction ltd. (Belgium v. Spain)* ICJ 1970, Second Phase ¶33. Emphasis added. Gill, ed. 158–160; Aceves, 357; Kadelbach, 27. de Hoogh (1991), however, did not find any support in the Court's dictum for any assertion of an *actio popularis*.

29. *Barcelona Traction* Second Phase ¶35.

30. Hillgruber, 267, n.8; de Hoogh (1991), 192.

31. Tams, 162. He goes on to note, however, that Judge Ammoun did explicitly reach this conclusion in his concurring separate opinion. Tams, 164.

32. Tams, 49–50.

33. Tams, 103–115. Other uses he identifies are precluding the territorial restriction of the application of a treaty, and "in a descriptive way, as a substitute for 'all States.' "

34. *Case Concerning East Timor (Portugal v. Australia)* ICJ 1995.

35. Christine Chinkin, "East Timor Moves into the World Court," *European Journal of International Law* 4 (1993): 211.

36. Vaughan Lowe, "The International Court in a Timorous Mood," *Cambridge Law Journal* 54 (1995): 484.

37. Christine Chinkin, "The East Timor Case (*Portugal v. Australia*)," *International and Comparative Law Quarterly* 45 (1996): 717.

38. *East Timor,* ¶23, 24.

39. *East Timor,* ¶26, 28; Gill, ed. 192–193; Lefeber, 4.

40. *Case Concerning East Timor* ¶29. Emphasis added.

41. Iain G.M. Scobbie and Catriona Drew, "Self-Determination Undermined: The Case of East Timor," *Leiden Journal of International Law* 9 (1996): 190.

42. Tams, 185.

43. Lowe, 484–486; Richard Burchill, "The ICJ Decision in the Case Concerning East Timor: The Illegal Use of Force Validated?" *Journal of Armed Conflict Law* 2 (1997): 1–16; Scobbie and Drew, 190–211.

44. *Monetary Gold Removed from Rome in 1943 (Italy v. France, United Kingdom and United States)*, ICJ, 1953; Lowe, 485; Gill, ed. 147–148.

45. Lowe, 485.

46. Chinkin (1996), 721–722.

47. Ragazzi, 212.

48. Hillgruber, 271–272.

49. Nigel White and Ademola Abass, "Countermeasures and Sanctions," in Malcolm Evans, ed., *International Law* 2nd ed. (Oxford: Oxford University Press, 2006), 514.
50. White and Abass are much less sanguine on this account. White and Abass, 517–521.
51. Tams, 210–225.
52. Tams, 225–227.
53. Tams, 230–231.
54. Hillgruber, 283; White and Abass, 520.
55. Christian Tomuschat, "Reconceptualizing the Debate on *Jus Cogens* and Obligations *Erga Omnes*—Concluding Observations," in Tomuschat and Thouvenin, eds. 429.
56. Gaja, 280–281; MacDonald, 137. Byers responds: "Although some of the rules which the Court identified as being *erga omnes* rules may also be considered *jus cogens* rules, the Court in this passage [the passage quoted above] was clearly referring to a characteristic distinct form that of non-derogability" Byers (1997), 230.
57. Hannikainen, 207; M. Sherif Bassiouni, "International Crimes: *Jus Cogens* and *Obligatio Erga Omnes*," *Law and Contemporary Problems* 59 (1996): 63, 65–66; Kadelbach, pp. 25–28.
58. Byers (1997): 230.
59. Byers (1997): 233.
60. Byers (1997): 212. Ragazzi provides a potential counterexample to Byers' first assertion in his postulate of regional *jus cogens*, but is unable to muster empirical support for such an entity. Ragazzi, 194–199.
61. Byers (1997): 236, 212–213; Tomushcat reaches the same conclusion at page 429.

Chapter 5

1. American Law Institute, *Restatement 3rd of the Foreign Relations Law of the United States* (1987), §404 and §404, Comment A.
2. Edward M. Wise, "Extradition: The Hypothesis of a *Civitas Maxima* and the Maxim *Aut Dedere Aut Judicare*," *Revue Internationale de Droit Penal*/International Review of Penal Law 62 (New Series) (1991): 109–133; Colleen Enache-Brown and Ari Fried, "Universal Crime, Jurisdiction and Duty: The Obligation of *Aut Dedere Aut Judicare* in International Law," McGill Law Journal/*Revue de Droit de McGill* 43 (1998): 613–633; M. Cherif Bassiouni, *Introduction to International Criminal Law* (Ardsley: Transnational Publishers, 2003), 334–346.

3. Jordan J. Paust et al., *International Criminal Law: Cases and Materials* 3rd (Durham: Carolina Academic Press, 2007), 155.

4. On the definition of the principle generally, see *inter alia Restatement* 3rd, §404; Thomas H. Sponsler, "The Universality Principle and the Threatened Trials of American Airmen," *Loyola Law Review* 15 (1968): 43–44; Kenneth C. Randall, "Universal Jurisdiction Under International Law," *Texas Law Review* 66 (1988): 788; Jon B. Jordan, "Universal Jurisdiction in a Dangerous World," *MSU-DCL Journal of International Law* 9 (2000): 3–5; Amnesty International, *Universal Jurisdiction: The Duty of States to Enact and Implement Legislation* (2001), Introduction, p. 1; chapter 1, 2, 11; Leila Nadya Sadat, "Redefining Universal Jurisdiction," *New England Law Review* 35 (2001): 246; Bartram S. Brown, "The Evolving Concept of Universal Jurisdiction," *New England Law Review* 35 (2001): 383–384; Luc Reydams, *Universal Jurisdiction: International and Municipal Legal Perspectives* (Oxford: Oxford University Press, 2003); Bruce Broomhall, *International Justice and the International Criminal Court* (Oxford: Oxford University Press, 2003), 106; Stephen Macedo, ed. *Universal Jurisdiction: National Courts and the Prosecution of Serious Crimes under International Law* (Philadelphia: University of Pennsylvania Press, 2004), 21 (Principle 1 of the Princeton Principles on Universal Jurisdiction); Yana Shy Kraytman, "Universal Jurisdiction—Historical Roots and Modern Implications," *BSIS Journal of International Studies* 2 (2005): 94–95; Beth van Schaack and Ronald C. Slye, *International Criminal Law and Its Enforcement: Cases and Materials* (New York: Foundation Press, 2007), 100; Alexander Zahar and Göran Sluiter, *International Criminal Law* (Oxford: Oxford University Press, 2008), 496; Florian Jessberger, "Universal Jurisdiction," in Antonio Cassese, ed., *The Oxford Companion to International Criminal Justice* (Oxford: Oxford University Press, 2009), 555–558.

5. M. Cherif Bassiouni, *Crimes Against Humanity in International Criminal Law* 2nd (Dordrecht: Kluwer Law International, 1999), 229.

6. Lowe (2006), 351–352; Wade Estey, "The Five Bases of Extraterritorial Jurisdiction and the Failure of the Presumption Against Extraterritoriality," *Hastings International and Comparative Law Review* 21 (1997–1998): 204.

7. Henry J. Steiner, "Three Cheers for Universal Jurisdiction—Or Is It Only Two?" *Theoretical Inquiries in Law* 5 (2004): 204.

8. M. Cherif Bassiouni, "Universal Jurisdiction for International Crimes: Historical Perspectives and Contemporary Practice," *Virginia Journal of International Law* 42 (2001): 88; 96. Sadat uses the phrase "humanity's agents." Sadat, 244. See also Schwelb, 46–56; Christopher C. Joyner, "Arresting Impunity: The Case for Universal Jurisdiction in Bringing War Criminals to Accountability," *Law and Contemporary Problems* 59 (1997): 169.

9. Rubin is strikingly deflationary in his assessment of the role that the idea of *actio popularis* played in the formulation of the UP. Rubin, 268; Andreas Zimmermann, "Violations of Fundamental Norms of International Law and the Exercise of Universal Jurisdiction in Criminal Matters," in Tomuschat and Thouvenin, eds. 337–339.

10. Gerhard Werle, *Principles of International Criminal Law* (Cambridge T.M.C. Asser Press, 2005), 58–59.

11. William Blackstone, *Commentaries on the Laws of England* v. 4 1769. p. 71. Quoted in Amnesty International (2001), chapter 2, 8–9, n. 26.

12. Amnesty International (2001), chapter 2, 1. They refer to heading C.3.15.1, *Ubi de criminibus agi oportet* (Where crimes should be tried), which states:

> It is well known that investigations of crimes, which are punished by the laws, or under the ordinary procedure, should be finished where the crimes have been committed or (the trial is) commenced, or where the persons who are said to be guilty are found.

From the Fred Blume translation found at uwacadweb.uwyo.edu/blume&justinian. Blume's exegetical note to this heading strongly undermines any link to the modern practice of universal jurisdiction. One obvious reason not to equate this with modern ideas of universality is that this was a domestic law, operative within a single, albeit imperial jurisdiction.

13. Willard B. Cowles, "Universality of Jurisdiction over War Crimes," *California Law Review* 33 (1945): 188–194; Sponsler, 44–45; Randall, 791–798; Estey, 195–196; Bassiouni (1999): 229; Jordan, 5; 10–12; Bassiouni (2001): 108–112; Amnesty International (2001), chapter 2, 3–9; Sadat, 244; Madeline H. Morris, "Universal Jurisdiction in a Divided World," *New England Law Review* 35 (2001): 339–340; Michael P. Scharf, "Application of Treaty-Based Universal Jurisdiction to Nationals of Non-Party States," *New England Law Review* 35 (2001): 369–370; Brown,

p. 384; Bruce Broomhall, "Toward the Development of an Effective System of Universal Jurisdiction for Crimes under International Law," *New England Law Review* 35 (2001): 402; Antonio Cassese, "Is the Bell Tolling for Universality? A Plea for a Sensible Notion of Universal Jurisdiction," *Journal of International Criminal Justice* 1 (2003): 284; Kraytman, 97–98.

The aptness of the canon's approach is certainly not without its detractors. Alfred P. Rubin, *The Law of Piracy* (Annapolis: Naval War College Press, 1988), 292–298; Alfred P. Rubin, *Ethics and Authority in International Law* (Cambridge: Cambridge University Press, 1997), 84–97; Rubin (2001): 267; Kraytman, 98–99; Eugene Kontorovich, "The Piracy Analogy: Modern Universal Jurisdiction's Hollow Foundation," *Harvard International Law Journal* 45 (2004): 183–237, *passim;* Gerry Simpson, "Piracy and the Origins of Enmity" in Matthew Craven, Malagosia Fitzmaurice and Maria Vogiatzi, eds. *Time, History and International Law* (Leiden: Martinus Nijhoff, 2007), 219–230.

14. This phrase can be traced back at least as far as Cicero's *De Officiis,* III.107.

15. Rubin (1988), citing Gentili, *Hispanicis Advocationis* (1613), I.IV.15.

16. Bassiouni (2001) and Simpson (2007) both note, however, that this was not the case in the ancient Greek and Roman worlds. Bassiouni (2001): 108; Simpson (2007), 228–229.

Rubin, however, suggests that the communities to which Bassiouni and Simpson refer did not fit our modern definition of pirates, and that lexical and orthographic similarities notwithstanding, the Greek and Latin words from which our term derives (*peirato* and its cognates and *pirata,* respectively) did not mean anything like what "pirate" today connotes. Rubin (1988), 3–13. He goes on to demonstrate that the passages from Classical Greek literature upon which they rely do not even use *peirato* or any of its cognates (although that is how the Greek terms have been translated).

17. *U.S. v. Smith* (1820) quoted in Scharf, 369. Spelling modernized.

18. *United States vs Brig Malek Adhel,* 43 U.S. (2 How.) 210, 232. 1844. Quoted in Randall, 794. Full text of quotation restored.

19. Bassiouni (1999): 229 and Randall, 791 both quote Oppenheim: "before International Law in the modern sense of the term was in existence, a pirate was already considered and outlaw, a '*hostis humani generis.*' " Lassa Oppenheim, *International Law: A Treatise* (8th ed. vol. 1, Hersch Lauterpacht, ed.) (New York: Longman,

Green, 1955), 609. Brierly goes so far as to label the practice "ancient." J.L. Brierly, *The Law of Nations* 6th ed. (Sir Humphrey Waldock, ed.) (Oxford: Oxford University Press, 1963), 311. As was the case with the purported acceptance of piracy in the ancient Greek world, Rubin likewise casts serious doubt on the original significance of this Ciceronian formulation. Rubin (1988), 10–12.

20. Randall, 791.
21. Thomson, 50–54; 107–118.
22. *Article 100—Duty to Cooperate in the Repression of Piracy* "All States shall cooperate to the fullest possible extent in the repression of piracy on the high seas or in any other place outside the jurisdiction of any State."
23. Kraytman, 97–98; Randall, 794–795; Georges Abi-Saab, "The Proper Role of Universals Jurisdiction," *Journal of International Criminal Justice* 1 (2003): 599.
24. Amnesty International (2001), chapters 2, 9; Abi-Saab demonstrates some affinity for this view.
25. Kontorovich makes a similar point. Kontorovich, 190.
    There is a related, but long-discredited view that by virtue of their activities, pirates were stateless persons aboard stateless ships, articulated *inter alia* in *U.S. v Klintock* (U.S. Supreme Court 1820). Cited in Scharf, 369. This would render Territorial and National jurisdiction inapplicable (although it would not bear on Passive Personality jurisdiction). This view is easily set aside because as a basic matter of the rules of nationality engaging in piracy cannot strip an individual's (or ship's) state of its jurisdiction over them. Randall, 794. This is reaffirmed in Article 104 of *UNCLOS*.
26. Scharf, 369; Joyner, 165, n. 48.
27. "Gravest crimes" formulation from Amnesty International, "Universal Jurisdiction: Questions and Answers" (2001a), 2; "shock the conscience" formulation from *The State of Israel v. Eichmann*, 1961, 45 P.M. 3, part II, paragraph 12; "sicken the conscience" and "universally abhorrent" formulations from Joyner, 153, 165.
28. Sadat, 244. "Crimes subject to the UP are so threatening to the international community or so heinous in scope and degree that they offend the interest of all humanity . . . ;" Scharf, 368. The *Restatement* (3rd) uses the rather less colorful phrase "recognized . . . as of universal concern." *Restatement* (3rd) §404.
29. Kontorovich, 185.
30. Quoted in Sponsler, 50.
31. 630 F.2d 876 (2nd Circuit 1980) 890.

32. Tellingly, Lowe, in disaggregating crimes of universal jurisdiction into "heinous crimes" and "crimes that are serious and which might otherwise go unpunished," puts piracy in the latter category. Lowe (2006), p. 348.

33. Thomson, 69–76.

34. It became clear that this is still a live issue with the proposal of H.R. 3216, *The Marque and Reprisal Act of 2007,* which sought to issue letters of Marque to private actors in furtherance of U.S. aims in the War on Terror.

35. Recall the qualification in Justice Story's definition of piracy: "without any . . . pretense of public authority."

36. *Leviathan,* II.XXIX.6–8.

37. Kontorovich, 210–217.

38. Kontorovich, 223–226; Rubin (1988), 122–275, *passim.*

39. Kontorovich, 92.

40. Byers (1999), 131; Jörg Kammerhofer, "Uncertainty in the Formal Sources of International Law: Customary International Law and Some of Its Problems," *European Journal of International Law* 15 (2003): 534–535; Ian Brownlie, "Methodological Problems in International Law and Development," *Journal of African Law* 26 (1982): 10.

41. Rubin (1997), 98, 108–124.

42. Amnesty International (2001), chapter 2, 10. Randall invokes the language of "heinousness." Randall, 800.

43. Kontorovich, however, reads the language of this treaty as using piracy merely "colloquially as a term of opprobrium for crime," but offers neither a historical nor a lexical basis for this assertion. Kontorovich, 193, n. 59; Randall, 800, n. 88; Bassiouni (2001): 112–113.

44. *Vienna Convention on the Law of Treaties* (1969), Art. 34; Anthony Aust, *Modern Treaty Law and Practice* 2nd (Cambridge: Cambridge University Press, 2000), 256–261; *Digest,* XLV.I.83.

45. He continues: "Contemporary lawyers would clearly have regarded such jurisdictional treaties as an acknowledgment of the absence of universal jurisdiction over slave trading." Kontorovich, 193–194.

46. Randall reads a form of universal jurisdiction in this regime inasmuch as there need be no link between the state exercising jurisdiction and the vessel and its crew engaging in the slave trade. Randall, 800. This stretches "universal" to the breaking point.

Paust captures the matter well in asserting that "universal jurisdiction" by treaty "is actually a form of consensual jurisdiction among the signatories." Paust, 155. Picking up the thread, Broomhall insists that, "this form of jurisdiction is not truly 'universal', but is a regime of rights and obligations arising among a closed set of parties." Broomhall (2003), 107. Jurisdiction *inter partes* can only be universal if membership is as well.

47. Bassiouni is simply materially incorrect in his assertion "A trial would...be held in the country which seized the vessel." Bassiouni, "Enslavement as an International Crime," *New York University Journal of International Law and Politics* 23 (1991): 461.

    If the language of Article VII left any ambiguity (it did not: "be taken into a port belonging to the nation of the *detained* vessel, to be there proceeded against"), Art. X surely clarified it in stating that the ship and crew were to be taken "before the competent Tribunals of the country to which she belongs." Were any uncertainty to linger, Annex B, in listing where ships of each nationality were to be brought for trial surely put an end to it, in each instance specifying *by name* French ports for French ships, British ports for British ships, et cetera.

48. Bassiouni (1991): 461.

49. Fischer, "The Suppression of Slavery in International Law (1)," *International Law Quarterly* 3 (1950): 45.

50. Hume, *A Treatise of Human Nature* III.I.I.27.

51. Kontorovich, 194.

52. Bassiouni (1990–1991): 445; Bassiouni (2001): 112; Kraytman, 100.

53. The body of §404 asserts that the slave trade is a universal jurisdiction crime; *Comment A* clarifies: "These offenses are subject to universal jurisdiction as a matter of customary law."

54. It must be noted that Higgins's assertion was not made in the course of a legal decision, but before joining the Court. It can be held neither to represent the sentiment of the Court, nor her position on the bench. Dame Rosalyn Higgins, *Problems and Process: International Law and How We Use It* (Oxford: Oxford University Press, 1994), 58.

55. Bassiouni (1990–1991): 445–449; Jordan, 12.

56. Randall, 799, fn. 79. Emphasis added.

57. For detailed discussions of the drafting, scope, and effect of the entire body of post – World War Two treaties purported to give rise to universal jurisdiction, see Randall, 816–829; 834–839;

Amnesty International (2001), chs. 3, 5, 7, 9, 11–13; Bassiouni (2001): 115–139; Bassiouni (2004): 52–61.

58. Bass (2000) discusses previous, frustrated twentieth-century attempts to bring war criminals and perpetrators of crimes against humanity to justice. Gary Bass, *Stay the Hand of Vengeance: The Politics of War Crimes Tribunals* (Princeton: Princeton University Press, 2000), 58–146, *passim*. For a defendant-by-defendant account of the proceedings at Nuremberg see Eugene Davidson, *The Trial of the Germans: An Account of the Twenty-Two Defendants before the International Military Tribunal at Nuremberg* (New York: Macmillan, 1966).

59. *Judgment of the International Military Tribunal for the Trial of German Major War Criminals:* The Law of the Charter, ¶3. Emphasis added.

King makes a great deal of scattered universal-sounding remarks in Justice Jackson's opening statement before the Tribunal, but we cannot make serious inference about the basis of the Tribunal's jurisdictional base from the oratory of the Prosecution. It must also be noted that reference to piracy at paragraph notwithstanding (and this in relation to *individual* rather than *universal* jurisdiction), Jackson does plainly root the Court's jurisdiction in the Charter, and the Charter's in the specific *inter partes* treaty obligations the accused were alleged to have violated. Henry T. King Jr., "Universal Jurisdiction: Myths, Realities, Prospects, War Crimes and Crimes Against Humanity: The Nuremberg Precedent," *New England Law Review* 35 (2001): 281–282.

60. Amnesty International (2001), chapter 2, 25–26.

61. *Judgment of the IMT:* The Law of the Charter, ¶1, 2.

62. Randall, 805.

63. Sponsler, 51; Randall, 805–806; Bassiouni (2001): 91, 118;

64. Randall, 808; Bassiouni (1999): 236; Amnesty International (2001), chapter 2, 27; King, 284.

65. Randall, 808; Bassiouni (1999): 236; Amnesty International (2001), chapter 2, 28. In this case, however, the British additionally had passive personality jurisdiction as the victims were British nationals.

66. Randall, 808–809; Amnesty International (2001), chapter 2, 28–29.

67. Randall, 809; Amnesty International (2001), chapter 2, 27–28.

68. Randall, 809–810; Bassiouni (1999): 236–237; Amnesty International (2001), chapter 2, 28.

69. Morris, 342. Like the British in *Almelo,* the French had passive personality jurisdiction in this case.
70. The story of Eichmann's crimes, his capture and trial are well documented; see *inter alia* Hannah Arendt, *Eichmann in Jerusalem: A Report on the Banality of Evil* (New York: Viking Press, 1964); Gideon Hausner, *Justice in Jerusalem* (New York: Harper & Row, 1966); Lord Russell of Liverpool, *The Record: The Trial of Adolf Eichmann for his Crimes against the Jewish People and against Humanity* (New York: Alfred P. Knopf, 1963).
71. *Attorney General of Israel v. Eichmann,* District Court of Jerusalem, Criminal Case No. 40/61, December 11, 1961.
72. *Attorney General of Israel v. Eichmann,* Supreme Court of Israel, Criminal Appeal No. 336/61, May 29, 1962.
73. *Nazis and Nazi Collaborators (Punishment) Law—5710/ 1950 §1(a).*
74. *Judgment* §§11–12.
75. *Appeal* §10; §11(b).
76. Randall, p. 811.
77. *Judgment* § 26; *Appeal* §10. Bass (2004) shares this conclusion, arguing that there is no significance to the "Crimes Against the Jewish People" / "Crimes Against Humanity" dichotomy. Gary Bass, "The Adolf Eichmann Case: Universal and National Jurisdiction," in Macedo, ed. 84–86.
78. Kontorovich, 96–197.
79. Former premier Hideki Tojo, prosecuted and convicted by the International Military Tribunal for the Far East after World War Two, was head of government; the Emperor of Japan was head of state. There is, as we shall see *infra* some dispute about the scope immunity *ratione personae* of a head of government who is not also a head of state; it was the position of Lord Millett in *Pinochet III* that it extended only to heads of state, but the majority in *Congo v Belgium* held that it extends to all ministers of government. In the case of Tojo, the matter was obviated by express provision of jurisdiction in Article 6 of the IMTFE's Charter.
80. *Regina v. Bartle et al. ex parte Pinochet,* Judgment of 25 November 1998 (*Pinochet I*); *in re Pinochet,* Judgment of 17 December 1998 (*Pinochet II*); *Regina v. Bartle, et al. ex parte Pinochet,* Judgment of 24 March 1999 (*Pinochet III*).
81. Chile, the United Kingdom and Spain are all parties to the 1984 *Convention Against Torture and other Cruel, Inhuman or Degrading Treatment or Punishment.*

82. Neil Boister and Richard Burchill, "The *Pinochet* Precedent: Don't Leave Home Without It," *Criminal Law Forum* 10 (1999): 412–413.

83. Lord Steyn, *Pinochet I.*

84. Henley, "Sovereignty, Augusto Pinochet, and Legal Positivism," *Human Rights Review* 8 (2006): 72–74.

85. Lord Nicholls, *Pinochet I.*

86. Lord Browne-Wilkinson, *Pinochet III.* Lord Hope of Craighead formulated his conclusion similarly: "[acts of torture] cannot be regarded as functions of a head of state under international law when international law expressly prohibits torture … in any circumstances whatsoever and had made it an international crime." Lord Hope of Craighead, *Pinochet III.*

87. Lord Millett, *Pinochet III.*

88. Lord Millett made the most expansive claims:

    In my opinion, crimes prohibited by international law attract universal jurisdiction under customary law if two criteria are satisfied. First, they must be contrary to a peremptory norm of international law so as to infringe a *jus cogens.* Secondly, they must be so serious and on such a scale that they can justly be regarded as an attack on the international order … Every state has jurisdiction under customary law to exercise extra-territorial jurisdiction in respect of crimes which satisfy the relevant criteria … the systematic use of torture … [has] joined piracy, war crimes and crimes against peace as an international crime of universal jurisdiction.

    He elaborated further in Lord Millett, "The *Pinochet* Case—Some Personal Reflections," in Malcolm Evans, ed., *International Law* 2nd ed. (Oxford: Oxford University Press, 2006), 9.

89. Naomi Roht-Arriaza, "The Pinochet Precedent and Universal Jurisdiction," *New England Law Review* 35 (2001): 313.

90. Amnesty International, *The Pinochet Case—Universal Jurisdiction and Absence of Immunity for Crimes Against Humanity* (1999), 10–12, 21–25. Familiarly, we find piracy analogy at work in the construction of their argument.

91. *Law of 16 June 1993 Relative to the Repression of Grave Violations of the Geneva Conventions and their First and Second Protocols.* This was amended in 1999 to include genocide and crimes against humanity in the *Law Relative to the Repression of Grave Violation of International Humanitarian Law.* The phrase is Cassese's. Antonio Cassese, "When May Senior State Officials Be Tried for International Crimes? Some Comments on the *Congo v. Belgium* Case," *European Journal of International Law* 13 (2002): 856.

92. *Case Concerning the Arrest Warrant of 11 April 2000 (Democratic Republic of the Congo v. Belgium)*, Judgment of 14 February 2002.
93. For a detailed history of changes to the Belgian legislation, see Luc Reydams, "Belgium Reneges on Universality: The 5 August 2003 Act on Grave Breaches of International Humanitarian Law," *Journal of International Criminal Law* 1 (2003a): 679–689; Steven R. Ratner, "Belgium's War Crimes Statute: A Postmortem," *American Journal of International Law* 97 (2003): 889–892; Tom Ongena and Ignace van Daele, "Universal Jurisdiction for International Core Crimes: Recent Developments in Belgium," *Leiden Journal of International Law* 15 (2002): 696–701. For detailed analysis of the legislation itself see Ongena and van Daele, 688–694; Reydams (2003), 102–109; Luc Reydams, "Universal Criminal Jurisdiction: The Belgian State of Affairs," *Criminal Law Forum* 11 (2000): 186–197. See Malvinia Halberstam, "Belgium's Universal Jurisdictional Law: Vindication of International Justice or Pursuit of Politics?" *Cardozo Law Review* 25 (2003): 247–266 for heated criticism of the Belgian law.
94. Reydams (2003), 106–107. The translation is Reydams'.
95. Ongena and van Daele, 691.
96. *Abbas Hijazi, et al. v Sharon, et al., Cour de Cassation,* decision of 12 February 2003. Reydamns (2003a): 680.
97. Reydams (2003), 107–108.
98. Reydams (2000): 190–191.
99. *Congo v. Belgium,* Judgment, ¶15. The quotation comes from Alexander Orakhelashvili, "Arrest Warrant of 11 April 2000 (Democratic Republic of the Congo v. Belgium)," *American Journal of International Law* 96 (2002): 677 (summary of the ICJ's decision).
100. *Congo v. Belgium,* Judgment, ¶1, 11, 12, 17.
101. *Congo v. Belgium,* Judgment, ¶21, 45.
102. *Congo v. Belgium,* Judgment, ¶43, 46.
103. *Congo v. Belgium,* Judgment, ¶54.
104. *Congo v. Belgium,* Judgment, ¶61. Emphasis added.
105. *Congo v. Belgium,* Separate Opinion of President Guillaume, ¶1.
106. *Congo v. Belgium,* Joint Separate Opinion of judges Higgins, Kooijmans, and Buergenthal, ¶3–5.
107. Cassese (2002): 855–856; Jan Wouters, "The Judgment of the International Court of Justice in the *Arrest Warrant* Case: Some Critical Remarks," *Leiden Journal of International Law* (2003): 263–264.

108. Inasmuch as this implies that the immunity (or the rule under-lying it) has *jus cogens* status, Stein points to the conclusion that either this is not the case or most of the treaties that form the International Criminal Law regime are void. Torsten Stein, "Limits of International Law Immunities for Senior State Officials in Criminal Procedure" in Christian Tomuschat and Jean-Marc Thouvenin, eds, *The Fundamental Rules of the International Legal Order: Jus Cogens and Obligations Erga Omnes* (Leiden: Martinus Nijhoff Publishers, 2006), 249.

109. Joint Separate Opinion, ¶81 "We have found no basis for the argument that Ministers of Foreign Affairs are entitled to the same immunities as heads of state"; ¶85 " . . . serious international crimes cannot be regarded as official acts"; *Congo v. Belgium,* Dissenting Opinion of Judge van den Wyngaert, ¶11–23 on immunity *ratione personae;* Cassese (2002): 862–874; Steffen Wirth, "Immunity for Core Crimes? The ICJ's Judgment in the *Congo v. Belgium* Case," *European Journal of International Law* 13 (2002): 883–891; Maria Spinedi, "State Responsibil-ity v. Individual Responsibility for International Crimes: *Tertium non Datur?" European Journal of International Law* 13 (2002): 897–899; Wouters, 262–263; Phillipe Sands, "International Law Transformed? From *Pinochet* to *Congo . . .?" Leiden Journal of International Law* 16 (2003): 49–53.

110. Wolfke is more cautious. Wolfke, 86–90.

111. Charney, however, in asserting the centrality of custom for the cre-ation of "universal international law," concludes that this principle is not recognized in international law. Jonathan Charney, "Univer-sal International Law," *American Journal of International Law* 87 (1993): 538–541.

112. Byers (1999), 77–78.

113. James Crawford, *The International Law Commission's Articles on State Responsibility: Introduction, Text, and Commentaries* (Cambridge: Cambridge University Press, 2002), 48.

114. *Ethiopia v South Africa; Liberia v South Africa,* 2nd Phase, Judgment, ¶88.

115. *International Covenant on Civil and Political Rights,* Art. 41 (a voluntary procedure dependent upon reciprocity and amenable only to conciliation, not binding, enforceable decision); *European Convention for the Protection of Human Rights and Fundamen-tal Freedoms,* Art. 33; *American Convention on Human Rights,* Art. 45 (procedure of the same character as that of the *ICCPR),*

Art. 62 (a voluntary and reciprocity-dependent procedures which does result in binding, enforceable decisions); *African Charter on Human and Peoples' Rights,* Art. 47 (this procedure does not require consent or reciprocity, but is also conciliatory in character).

116. Randall, 789–790. He does concede, however, that third states are probably not under the formal *obligation* to prosecute or extradite. Randall, 823.

117. Broomhall (2001): 401.

Chapter 6

1. Nicholas Onuf, *World of Our Making* (Columbia: University of South Carolina Press, 1989); Onuf, "Constructivism: A User's Manual," in Vendulka Kubálkova, Nicholas Onuf and Paul Kowert, eds, *International Relations in a Constructed World* (Armonk: M.E. Sharpe, 1998), 58–78.

2. Alexander Wendt, *Social Theory of International Politics* (Cambridge: Cambridge University Press, 1999), 193–245; Patrick Thaddeus Jackson, "Is the State a Person? Why Should We Care?" *Review of International Studies* 30 (2004): 255–258; Iver Neumann, "Beware of Organicism: The Narrative Self of the State," *Review of International Studies* 30 (2004): 259–267; Colin Wight, "State Agency: Social Action without Human Activity?" *Review of International Studies* 30 (2004): 269–280; Patrick Thaddeus Jackson, "Hegel's House, or 'People are States Too'," *Review of International Studies* 30 (2004a): 281–287; Alexander Wendt, "The State as Person in International Theory," *Review of International Studies* 30 (2004): 289–316; Peter Lomas, "Anthropomorphism, Personification and Ethics: A Reply to Alexander Wendt," *Review of International Studies* 31/2 (2005): 349–355; Alexander Wendt, "How Not to Argue Against State Personhood: A Reply to Lomas," *Review of International Studies* 31 (2005): 357–360.

3. David Miller has posed complementary questions regarding the responsibility of nations. David Miller, "Holding Nations Responsible," *Ethics,* 114 (2004): 240–268. Toni Erskine, however, has explicitly rejected the inclusion of nations as "moral agents." Toni Erskine, "Assigning Responsibilities to Institutional Moral Agents: The Case of States and Quasi-States," *Ethics and International Affairs,* 15 (2001): 72.

4. As Kelsen has stated the issue; "The question whether a certain behavior, particularly whether a certain act, a certain function is

an act or function of the state, that is, whether it is the state as a person that performs an act or exercises a function, is not a question directed toward the existence of a fact … If the question did have this meaning, it could never be answered affirmatively. For in fact it is never the state but always a certain individual who is acting." Kelsen (1967), p. 291.

5. Samuel Pufendorf, *De Jure Naturae et Gentium Libro Octo*, I.1.13; *De Officio Hominis et Civis Libro Duo*, II.6.10. The issue is also treated in David Boucher, "Resurrecting Pufendorf and Capturing the Westphalian Moment," *Review of International Studies*, 27 (2001): 566–567. Jean-Jacques Burlamaqui basically restates the Hobbes—Pufendorf position: *The Principles of Natural and Political Law*, II.6.iv.

6. G.W.F. Hegel, "Philosophy of Right and Law," in Carl J. Friedrich, ed., *The Philosophy of Hegel* (New York: Random House, 1954), 320.

7. *Articles on Responsibility of States for Wrongful Acts*. Arts. 4–11; James Crawford, *The International Law Commission's Articles on State Responsibility* (Cambridge: Cambridge University Press, 2002), 91–123; James Crawford and Simon Olleson, "The Nature and Forms of International Responsibility," in Malcolm Evans, ed., *International Law* (Oxford: Oxford University Press, 2006), 454–458; Hans Kelsen, *Pure Theory of Law* 2nd ed. (Clark: The Lawbook Exchange, Ltd., 2005 (1967)), 292; Hans Kelsen, *General Theory of Law and State* (New Brunswick: Transaction Publishers, 1949 (2006)), 106.

8. Nina Jørgensen, *The Responsibility of States for International Crimes* (Oxford: Oxford University Press, 2000), 79, 279–280.

9. In the ICJ's recent *Genocide Case* for example the Court clearly stated that even in the case of Genocide, the responsibility of a state would not be criminal in nature. *Case Concerning the Application of the Convention on the Prevention and Punishment of the Crime of Genocide* ¶167.

10. The definitive account is to be found in Marina Spinedi, "International Crimes of State: The Legislative History," in Joseph Weiler, Antonio Cassese and Marina Spinedi, eds, *International Crimes of State: A Critical Analysis of the ILC's Draft Article 19 on State Responsibility* (New York: Walter de Gruyter, 1989), 7–138. Crawford (2002), 16–20 provides detailed discussion of the flaws in Article 19's framing that contributed to its exclusion. See also Jørgensen, *The Responsibility of States*, XI-XV, 175–184; and the essays by Abi-Saab, Graefrath, Dupuy, Stein, Cassese, Aldrich,

and Sinclair in Weiler et al. *International Crimes of States.* For a contrasting account, see Luis Molina, "Can States Commit Crimes? The Limits of Formal International Law," in Ross, ed., *Controlling State Crime* (New Brunswick: Transaction Publishers, 2000), 349–388.

11. Georges Abi-Saab, "The Uses of Article 19," *European Journal of International Law* 10 (1999): 345–346. Wyler, however, asserts "According to many commentators, the distinction introduced in Article 19 . . . between 'crimes' and 'delicts' led to a 'criminalization' of responsibility." Eric Wyler, "From 'State Crime' to Responsibility for Serious Breaches of Obligations under Peremptory Norms of General International Law," *European Journal of International Law* 13 (2002): 1148.

12. Alain Pellet, "Can a State Commit a Crime? Definitely, Yes!" *European Journal of International Law* 10 (1999): 432.

13. Giorgio Gaja, "Should all References to International Crimes Disappear from the ILC Draft Articles on State Responsibility?" *European Journal of International Law* 10 (1999), 365.

14. Crawford (2002), 19.

15. Mortimer Sellers, "International Legal Theory," *Jus Gentium* 11 (2005): 67.

16. On the nature of legal fictions, see: Lon L. Fuller, Legal Fictions (Stanford: Stanford University Press, 1967); Sanford Schane, "The Corporation is a Person: The Language of a Legal Fiction," *Tulane Law Review* 61 (1987); Note, "What We Talk About When We Talk About Persons: The Language of A Legal Fiction," *Harvard Law Review* 114 (2001): 1750–1754.

17. P.W. Duff, *Personality in Roman Law* (Cambridge: Cambridge University Press, 1938), 28.

18. Peter French, *Collective and Corporate Persons* (New York: Columbia University Press, 1984), 34; Duff, 21, 35, 50, 72, 223; Andrew Borkowski and Paul du Plessis, *Textbook on Roman Law* 3rd ed. (Oxford: Oxford University Press, 2005), 87; Barry Nicholas, *An Introduction to Roman Law* (Oxford: Oxford University Press, 1996 (1962)), 60.

    Malmendier—based upon a nonjuridical source, Cicero's *Epistulae Ad Familiares* 13.9.2—asserts that there was a particular class of *corpus,* the *societas publicanorum,* to which the Romans granted *personam.* Close examination of Cicero's original text does not bear this out. Ulrike Malmendier, "Roman Shares," in William N. Goetzman and K. Gert Rouwenhorst, eds, *The Origins of Value* (Oxford: Oxford University Press, 2005), 38; Cicero, *Epistulae Ad Familiares* 13.9.2.

19. Duff, 21, 26 commenting on Ulpian in D.4.2.9.1.
20. Duff, 33. Oakeshott famously also includes *societates*, associations of "individuals each of whom conditions his actions to accord with the terms of a joint agreement." Michael Oakeshott, "On the Character of a Modern European State," in Michael Oakeshott, ed., *On Human Conduct* (Oxford: Oxford University Press, 1975), 199–266. *Societas* is also Malmendier's preferred category term.
21. Duff, 33, 50, 62, 70, 172; Malmendier, 6; Wolff (1951), 235.
22. Compare Duff, 37, 72 with Malmendier, 36.
23. Duff, 171, 175.
24. Hale cites similar passages from I Corinthians 12:12–27. David G. Hale, "Analogy of the Body Politic," in Philip Wiener, ed., *Dictionary of the History of Ideas*, volume 1 (New York: Scribner & Sons. 1974), 68–70.
25. Ernst H. Kantorowicz, *The King's Two Bodies* (Princeton: Princeton University Press, 1997 (1957)), 195–196; Anton-Herman Chroust, "The Corporate Idea and the Body Politic in the Middle Ages," *The Review of Politics* 9 (1947): 431.
26. Cited in Kantorowicz, 194.
27. Chroust documents similar accounts in Remigio de' Girolami and Augustinus Triumphus of Ancona. Chroust, 432–433.
28. Kantorowicz, 200–202.
29. *Judgment of the International Military Tribunal for the German Major War Criminals*, Cmd. 6964, at 41. Cited in Jan Klabbers, "The Concept of Legal Personality," *Jus Gentium* 11 (2005): 45.
30. Crawford and Olleson, 460.
31. Hale, 68–70.
32. Kantorowicz, 210.
33. Kantorowicz, 212–223.
34. Chroust, 445, 447.
35. Chroust, 441.
36. Hannah Pitkin, "Hobbes's Concept of Representation—I," *American Political Science Review* 58 (1964): 328–340; Hannah Pitkin, "Hobbes's Concept of Representation—II," *American Political Science Review* 58 (1964): 902–918; Quentin Skinner, "Hobbes and the Purely Artificial Person of the State," in Quentin Skinner, *Visions of Politics v. III: Hobbes and Civil Science* (Cambridge: Cambridge University Press, 2002), 177–208; Quentin Skinner, "Hobbes on Representation," *European Journal of Philosophy* 13 (2005): 155–184. See also, *inter alia,* David Runciman, *Pluralism and the Personality of the State* (Cambridge: Cambridge University Press, 1997), 6–33, David Runciman, "Moral Responsibility and the Problem of Representing the State,"

in Toni Erskine, ed., *Can Institutions Have Responsibilities? Collective Moral Agency and International Relations* (Basingstoke: Palgrave, 2003), 41–48, and David Copp, "Hobbes on Artificial Persons and Collective Action," *The Philosophical Review*, 89 (1980): 579–606.

37. Thomas Hobbes, *Human Nature* XIX.7; *De Cive* V.7; *Leviathan* Introduction.

38. Skinner (2002), 197.

39. Hobbes, *Human Nature* XIX.10; the quoted phrase Skinner takes from Cicero's "*De Officis*" I.34. Skinner (2002), 199.

40. Skinner (2002), 192–193.

41. Hobbes, *Leviathan* I.XVI.1–3; *De Homine* XV.1.

42. Hobbes, *Leviathan* I.XVI.13; *De Homine* XV.2.

43. Hobbes, *Leviathan* I.XVI.4.

44. Hobbes, *De Corpore Politico* XX.2; *De Cive* V.9; *Leviathan* I.XVI.14; *De Homine* XV.2.

45. Hobbes, *De Corpore Politico* XX.2; *Leviathan* I.XVI.5; *De Homine* XV.2.

46. Torbjørn Knutsen, *A History of International Relations Theory* 2nd ed. (Manchester: Manchester University Press. 1997), 105.

47. Hobbes, *De Cive* V.9; *Leviathan* I.XVI.13–14.

48. Hobbes, *Leviathan* I.XVI.13.

49. Hobbes, *Leviathan* I.XVII.13.

50. Hobbes, *De Cive* VI.19.

51. Hobbes, *Leviathan* I.XVI.5. Emphasis added.

52. Hobbes, Leviathan I.XV.36; Richard Flathman, *Thomas Hobbes: Skepticism, Individuality and Chastened Politics* (London: Sage, 1993), 56–57; Kinch Hoekstra, "Hobbes on the Natural Condition of Mankind," in Patricia Springborg, ed., *The Cambridge Companion to Hobbes' Leviathan* (Cambridge: Cambridge University Press, 2007), 120–121. May seeks to undermine the significance of this distinction. Larry May, *Crimes Against Humanity: A Normative Account* (Cambridge: Cambridge University Press, 2005), 17–18.

53. Richard Tuck, *The Rights of War and Peace* (Cambridge: Cambridge University Press, 1999), 158–165.

54. Runciman seems to disagree with this conclusion. Runciman (2003) 48.

   May offers a reading of Hobbes that lends support for the idea of International Criminal Law, but he does so at the cost of completely eliding Hobbes's nominalism, and offers no indication that either he or Hobbes envisions *states* ever being criminal.

Just the opposite, he reminds us that notional body of the state is only an "outline," and redirects attention to the individual people composing it. May (2005), 15–16.

55. Arthur Machen, "Corporate Personality," *Harvard Law Review* 24 (1911): 263. Emphasis added.

56. Kelsen (1967), 178.

57. Mark M. Hager, "Bodies Politic: The Progressive History of Organizational 'Real Entity' Theory," *University of Pittsburgh Law Review* 50 (1989): 578. John Dewey tried to set aside the debate, and H.L.A. Hart also tried to move jurisprudence beyond the question "what is a corporation." John Dewey, "The Historic Background of Corporate Legal Personality," *Yale Law Journal* 35 (1926): 655; H.L.A. Hart, "Definition and Theory in Jurisprudence," in H.L.A. Hart, *Ethics in Jurisprudence and Philosophy* (Oxford: Clarendon Press, 1983), 43.

58. Frederic Maitland, "Moral Personality and Legal Personality," *Journal of the Society of Comparative Legislation* 6 (New Series) (1905), 195. Both Laufer and Horwitz identify this position less with nominalism than methodological individualism. William S. Laufer, *Corporate Bodies and Guilty Minds* (Chicago: The University of Chicago Press, 2006), 11. Morton Horwitz, *The Transformation of American Law 1870–1960: The Crisis of Legal Orthodoxy* (Oxford: Oxford University Press, 1992), 72.

59. Machen, 255.

Contrast Schane's account: "Legal relations . . . take place between one person and another. Now, individuals may enter into an association, but the resulting group has no independent existence . . . and unlike a natural person, it has no preexisting rights. Only in contemplation of the law does it become a legal entity—a *persona ficta*—an artificial, moral or juristic person" Schane, 565.

60. Machen, 257; Hager, 580.

61. Schane, 566.

62. Morris Cohen, "Communal Ghosts and Other Perils in Social Philosophy," *The Journal of Philosophy, Psychology and Scientific Methods* 16 (1919): 678–681; Laufer, 47.

63. Harold Laski, "The Personality of Associations," *Harvard Law Review* 29 (1916): 406.

64. Ernst Freund, *The Legal Nature of Corporations* (Chicago: University of Chicago Press, 1897), 52. Quoted in Borkowski, 102.

65. Laski, 406. Emphasis added.

Compare Lord Reid's 1972 decision in the *Tesco Supermarkets* Case, "A living person has a mind which can have knowledge or intention or be negligent and he has hands to carry out his intentions. A corporation has none of these," which illustrates the longevity of this view. Eric Colvin, "Corporate Personality and Criminal Liability," *Criminal Law Forum* 6 (1995): 5.

66. "A corporation exists as an objectively real entity...the law merely recognizes and gives legal effect to the existence of the entity. To confound legal recognition of existing facts with creation of facts is an error...A corporation is an entity—not imaginary or fictitious, but real, not artificial, but natural" Machen, 156, 161–162. Emphasis added. On Gierke generally, see Runciman (1977), 34–63.

67. Colvin, 2.

68. Machen, 161–162.

69. Ann Foerschler, "Corporate Criminal Intent: Toward a Better Understanding of Corporate Misconduct," *California Law Review* 78 (1990): 1291; Hart (1983), 45.

70. Laski, 413–415.

71. Jørgensen, 75; Lee, 9; R.E. Ewin, "The Moral Status of the Corporation," *Journal of Business Ethics* 10 (1991): 749–752. This is, of course, the model that international law follows in the Act of State Doctrine.

72. Colvin, 2; Radin, 663.

73. Colvin, 1–2. Compare Kelsen: "It is the action or refrainment from action by an individual that is interpreted as the action or refrainment of the corporation—'attributed' to the corporation. The human being through whom the corporation acts as a juristic person, and whose behavior is attributed to the corporation, is called the 'organ' of the corporation." Hans Kelsen (1967), 175, see also pages 177 and181 where Kelsen ultimately concludes, however, that juristic persons are "not capable of committing a delict." Earlier, however, Kelsen was willing to grant juristic persons the capacity to commit both civil and criminal delicts. Kelsen (1949), 103–106.

74. Colvin, 8–9. Emphasis added. This decision actually resembles what Jørgensen (following Andrews) calls the "Identification Theory"; in it the "basis for liability is that the acts of certain person are actually the acts of the corporation. 'These people are not seen as the agents of the company, but as its very person, and their guilt is the guilt of the company.' " Jørgensen, 75 quoting J. Andrews, "Reform in the Law of Corporate Liability" *Criminal Law Review* 20 (1973): 91–92.

75. Larry May, *The Morality of Groups* (South Bend: University of Notre Dame Press, 1987) 41.

76. May (1987), 91.

77. This is taken from *American Medical Association v. US* (1942) cited in Foerschler, "Corporate Criminal Intent," 1291.

78. Celia Wells, *Corporations and Criminal Responsibility* 2nd ed. (Oxford: Oxford University Press, 2001), 71. Wells quotes Brent Fisse and John Braithwaite, "The Allocation of Responsibility for Corporate Crime: Individualism, Collectivism and Accountability" *Sydney Law Review* 11 (1988): 483.

79. Erskine (2001), 70–72.

80. French, 39.

81. French, 42.

82. Foerschler, 1302–1303. Clarkson's approach is similar. C.M.V. Clarkson, "Kicking Corporate Bodies and Damning Their Souls," *The Modern Law Review* 59 (1996): 557–572.

83. Colvin, 24.

84. Colvin, 33–34.

85. Laufer, 77–83. Emphasis added.

86. Colvin, 40.

87. Cohen, 681.

88. Machen, 165.

89. Colvin, 15. Emphasis added.

90. Radin, 661. Emphasis added.

91. French, 188; Clarkson, 563.

92. Lang offers one account of how this might be justified. Anthony Lang, "Crime and Punishment: Holding States Accountable" *Ethics and International Affairs* 21 (2007): 239–257.

93. Donald Davidson, "Intending," in Davidson, *Essays on Actions and Events* (Oxford: Oxford University Press, 1980), 83–102.

94. Malcolm addresses Hobbes's relationship with the Reason of State literature. Noel Malcolm, *Reason of State, Propaganda, and the Thirty Years' War* (Oxford: Clarendon Press, 2007), 92–123.

95. Maurizio Viroli, *From Politics to Reason of State* (Cambridge: Cambridge University Press, 1992); Richard Tuck, *Philosophy and Government: 1572–1651* (Cambridge: Cambridge University Press, 1993), 31–64; Peter Burke, "Tacitism, Scepticism, and Reason of State," in J.H. Burns and Mark Goldie, eds., *The Cambridge History of Political Thought 1450 -1700* (Cambridge: Cambridge University Press, 1991), 479–498; Edward Keene, *International Political Thought: A Historical Introduction* (Cambridge: Polity

Press, 2005), 98–118; Jonathan Haslam, *No Virtue Like Necessity: Realist Thought in International Relations since Machiavelli* (New Haven: Yale University Press, 2002), 17–88.

96. Wendt (2004), 306–311.
97. Amy E. Eckert, "Peoples and Persons: Moral Standing, Power, and the Equality of States," *International Studies Quarterly* 50 (2006): 841–859; Amy E. Eckert, "National Defense and State Personality," *Journal of International Political Theory* 5 (2009), 161–176.
98. Eckert (2009), 167.
99. Eckert (2009), 167.
100. Eckert (2009), 168.
101. Eckert (2009), 170.
102. Kelsen (1967), 356; cf. 106.

    This position represents a complete reversal of his earlier arguments. Writing about the prosecutions after World War Two, he stated, "If it is possible to impute physical acts performed by individuals to the State although the State has no body, it must be possible to impute psychic acts to the State although the State has no soul." Hans Kelsen, "Collective and Individual Responsibility in International Law with Particular Respect to the Punishment of War Criminals" *California Law Review* 31 (1942–1943): 530, 533. Quoted in Jørgensen, *The Responsibility of States*, 281.
103. Maitland, 200 offers a similar formulation.
104. Jorgensen, 170–171.
105. Hugo Grotius, *De Jure Belli ac Pacis,* II.21.7.2 quoted in Lang, "Crime and Punishment," 15.

Index